An American Demonology

Flying Saucers Over The White House

*The story of Captain Edward J. Ruppelt
and Project Blue Book, the official UFO
investigation of the United States Air Force*

Colin Bennett

critical vision — an imprint of headpress

A Critical Vision Book
Published in 2005
by Headpress

Headpress/Critical Vision
PO Box 26
Manchester
M26 1PQ
United Kingdom

[tel] +44 (0)161 796 1935
[fax] +44 (0)161 796 9703
[email] info@headpress.com
[web] www.headpress.com

An American Demonology
Text copyright © Colin Bennett
This volume copyright © 2005 Headpress
Cover, layout & design: Walt Meaties & David Kerekes
World Rights Reserved

British Library Cataloguing in Publication Data
A catalogue record for this book is available from the British Library

ISBN 1-900486-46-6
EAN 9781900486460

www.headpress.com

A Chain of Being: The Cosmos of the Military Industrial Complex

A Set Of Correspondences: The Escher-Penrose Event

A Dance: UFOs over Washington

Appendix

For George Hanson,
author of *The Trickster and the Paranormal*

With thanks to Michael D. Hall & Wendy A. Connors,
authors of *Summer of the Saucers*

In studying Shakespeare's Histories I concluded that the pictures
of civil war and disorder they present had no meaning apart from
a background of order to judge them by. I found that the order I
was describing was much more than political order, or, if political,
was always a part of a larger cosmic order. I found, further, that the
Elizabethans saw this single order under three aspects: a chain, a set of
correspondences, and a dance.

E.M.W. Tillyard
Preface to *The Elizabethan World Picture*

...the orb-like lights came right at Patterson and clustered around his
aircraft. Desperate for a course of action, Patterson radioed ARTC
(Airport Radar Traffic Control) for assistance. He simply did not know
what to do. There was stunned silence among the tower personnel
at that moment. No one could say a word. Patterson was on his own.
Fortunately, the orbs then pulled away from Patterson's aircraft.

Summer of the Saucers
by Michael D. Hall and Wendy A. Connors

Introduction
by Nick Pope

THE BOOK YOU ARE about to read is the story of a hero and because all heroes must have a quest, it is also the story of his quest. The quest was a noble one and massive in scale: to investigate the UFO phenomenon for the United States Government, to see whether there was evidence of any threat to national security. The hero in this quest is Edward J. Ruppelt, a United States Air Force officer who from 1951 to 1953 headed Project Blue Book, the USAF's UFO project. An interesting fact, little known outside ufology (and not as widely known inside ufology as one would hope and expect) is that Ruppelt invented the term "unidentified flying object," which was to render virtually obsolescent the previous term, "flying saucer." Ruppelt undertook his investigations with diligence and professionalism, examining sightings from the public and the military alike, without fear, prejudice or preconceptions. While he knew, intellectually, that most UFO sightings were likely to be misidentifications of ordinary objects or phenomena, he went where the data took him and did not close his mind to the more exotic possibilities — and make no mistake, the historical record clearly shows that many within the government and military believed some UFOs were extraterrestrial in origin. Sightings from pilots and UFOs tracked on radar were of particular interest, but Ruppelt had to contend with something far more challenging than UFOs — he had to contend with the politics of ufology. Accordingly, Ruppelt's story is the story not just of investigating some of the world's most fascinating UFO encounters, but of his heroic attempts to steer a path between the competing demands of his military superiors, witnesses, the UFO lobby and the press. Ruppelt played a straight bat amidst the competing agendas and thus found his words and his views being twisted to fit the needs of others. In truth, he was neither diehard skeptic nor wide-eyed believer, though various factions have tried to portray him as a standard bearer for their respective belief systems. His position in the military limited his options for correcting all of this and it was only after he left the USAF that he was able to set out his side of the story. This he did in his 1956 book *The Report on Unidentified Flying Objects*. The

5

book's importance cannot be overstated and in my opinion it remains, to this day, the most significant book on the subject ever written. Ruppelt was portrayed as a maverick for having written the book, then further criticised for an updated version of his book, published in 1960, which toned down his original views on the subject. A good hero will, at some time, manage to upset just about everyone. Had he become disillusioned by some of the apparently wild claims of people claiming contact with aliens, had he (or his new employers, the Northrop Corporation) been "got at" by the government and forced to tone things down, or were his words being manipulated by his publishers? The debate continues to this day, as debates continue over the lives of most heroes, who are, by their nature, controversial figures. Ruppelt died of a heart attack in 1960 at the tragically young age of thirty five, thus fulfilling another heroic archetype. This untimely death robbed ufology of the one man who had the credentials and the integrity to turn ufology from a mystery into an emerging science, had he been minded so to do. However, one suspects that the politics that bedevilled him while stewarding Project Blue Book would have followed him into civilian ufology, had he chosen to become involved. But these are unknowns, just as the subject of his quest — the UFOs themselves — are still unknowns. And so Ruppelt remains the Establishment maverick. A gamekeeper, turned poacher, turned game-keeper again, whose life has largely been forgotten by a public whose new heroes are the "stars" of reality television shows. Colin Bennett's book is therefore most timely, as it turns the spotlight back, deservedly, on a real hero. If Ruppelt was a maverick, then so is his biographer. Colin Bennett is no stranger to controversy. His reinterpretation of ufology in terms of postmodernism has brought him opprobrium from skeptics and only a half-hearted welcome from believers. Like his hero, Bennett occasionally manages to upset everybody. But sacred ufological cows occasionally need to be slaughtered before they go mad, while those who have made so much from the subject cannot complain when they are cast out from the temple of ufology. Bennett has done ufology a wonderful service with this long overdue biography of one of ufology's Founding Fathers, and perhaps its greatest hero. Bennett's prose is colourful and vivid, his use of metaphor astounding. He thus resurrects not only Ruppelt, but also the quaint and quirky America of the fifties in which he lived. Moreover, he makes us mourn the passing of both the hero and his world. But while Ruppelt and his world belong to the past, the demons of Bennett's Demonology are still with us — as you are about to discover.

Nick Pope
UFO Desk Officer, UK Ministry of Defence, 1991–1994

Foreword
by Jerome Clark

EDWARD J. RUPPELT entered my life in October 1957. He has been there ever since, and if you are reading these words, chances are he is in yours.

In my young, impressionable days, Doubleday and Company, the venerable American publisher, ran the Science Fiction Book Club. Sometime in mid 1957, seeing an ad for the club on the back cover of a pulp SF zine, I took advantage of an introductory offer within my modest youthful price range: three titles for ninety nine cents. I vaguely recall the two other books — I think they were two fat anthologies, *Omnibus of Science Fiction* and *A Treasury of Science Fiction Classics* (I still have them somewhere, though I have not read SF in years) — and I'm sure they thrilled me even as their contents are a blur in five-decade-old recollection.

The third book, on the other hand ... I don't know why I chose it, except that the subject matter sounded intriguing. I knew of "flying saucers," of course. You couldn't be an American kid in the 1950s without having heard about them. I think I even remember when I was introduced to the concept, when our family — like nearly all American families back then — got its weekly issue of *Life*. This would have been the April 7, 1952, issue, with the classic article by H. B. Darrach, Jr., and Robert E. Ginna, Jr., "Have We Visitors from Space?" A few hours or days later, I told some playmates about "flying saucers." "Some people think they're from outer space," I said — something my dad must have told me, since I could not have read the piece myself. A year or so later, I saw a trailer for *Invaders from Mars*, and even this abbreviated view of that saucer-fiction film was sufficient to give me a UFO abduction nightmare so terrifying that it chills me still.

None of this prepared me, however, for the odd thrill I felt when that early autumn day, a few weeks away from my eleventh birthday, I picked up *The Report on Unidentified Flying Objects* for the first time and read, "This is a book about unidentified flying objects — UFOs — 'flying saucers.'" A delicious shudder, a spine tingling unease, passed through me. I read all the way through the foreword, on to the penultimate paragraph with the ultimate question: "What constitutes proof? Does a UFO have to land at the River Entrance to the Pentagon, near the Joint Chiefs of Staff offices? Or is it proof when a ground radar station detects a UFO, sends a jet to intercept it, the jet pilot sees it, and locks on with his radar, only to have the UFO streak away at a phenomenal speed?" And from there to the first chapter, with its irresistible first sentence: "In the summer of 1952 a United States Air Force F-86 jet interceptor shot at a flying saucer." Pulse quickening, eyes wide open, flashlight shining under bed sheets long past bedtime on the book's last words:

> Maybe the final proven answer will be that all of the UFOs that have been reported are merely misidentified known objects. Or maybe the many pilots, radar specialists, generals, industrialists, scientists, and the man on the street who have told me, "I wouldn't have believed it if I hadn't seen it myself," knew what they were talking about. Maybe the earth is being visited by interplanetary spaceships. Only time will tell.

Every one of us who lived through that decade has his or her private 1950s. Though the decade was more than half over before my eyes fell on those words, they are my private 1950s. They changed my life in all sorts of unanticipated ways for good and ill, though in all ways they made that life an interesting one, fueled by an ever deepening skepticism of received wisdom about all things, informed by the understanding that such wisdom has been so unwise about UFOs. After Ruppelt, planets and stars — which had lured me into my backyard nearly every unclouded evening with the 32 x reflecting telescope in which I had invested my meager paperboy's earnings — were no substitute for the more immediate and closer phenomena darting silently through our own atmosphere. What if the stars and planets weren't out there but, in some sense, *here*?

In my adolescence I read and reread Ruppelt, imagining myself in his shoes, even anticipating that one day I would join the US Air Force and become an officer who would be loyal, efficient, sharp, and affable like my hero. Meanwhile, as he would do to so many others through no intention of his own, Ruppelt led me to other ufology. Barely a month after I'd finished his book for that first time, newspapers all over the country — including the one I delivered after school every day — were reporting in headlined dispatches on the now classic American UFO wave of November 1957.

From there it was on to Charles Fort, then to Donald Keyhoe and George Adamski (where I had my first close encounter, with many more ahead of me, with a story that I flat out disbelieved). Then it was membership in Keyhoe's loftily monikered, Blue Book baiting National Investigations Committee on Aerial Phenomena (NICAP), followed by subscriptions to *Fate*, *Flying Saucer Review* and *Flying Saucers*, and discovery of the subculture of ufologists. Eventually, I would meet most of the famous ufologists and many of the pivotal witnesses (including Kenneth Arnold, whose June 1947 sighting started it all and with whom I was friendly in his last years). I would write my own books, most notably the multivolume *UFO Encyclopedia* (in two editions, 1990–1996, 1998).

I owe it all to Ruppelt who, as heroes are wont to do, would at last break my heart. In 1960 the notorious "second edition" of *Report* was published: three new chapters which drearily echoed the Air Force line that ostensible UFO sightings are all explainable, or potentially so; those who think otherwise are fools, misfits and dimwits, and those who are none of these can only be charlatans. Like many others I was stunned and hurt. Being young, I took it as a kind of personal betrayal. Still, when Ruppelt died later that same year — I learned of his passing in a brief note on a back page of NICAP's *U.F.O. Investigator* (the modest attention surely a consequence of Keyhoe's own bruised feelings) — I felt real grief.

These many years later, we know far more than we knew then, if not about UFOs as such then certainly about the events Ruppelt was recounting for the first time. We now know, for instance, that Ruppelt was always more skeptical than the first edition would lead one to believe. Left to his own devices, freed from commercial considerations and advice from his editor (some say ghostwriter) Jim Phelan, perhaps he would have written a book more to the liking of the Blue Book UFOphobes who followed him and some of whom remained his friends — though Ruppelt, to his credit, also stayed on cordial terms with pro-UFO associates such as Al Chop and Dewey Fournet.

In any event, it is almost certainly untrue, as has sometimes been speculated, that Ruppelt was "pressured" into writing the three new chapters. To every available appearance, they express views that he had held privately for some time. Ruppelt's best informed (and most vociferous) critic, Brad Sparks, correctly remarks, "Ruppelt defenders … tend to ignore Ruppelt's many extremely negative comments about UFOs, both public and private, which seem to overwhelm the very few mildly favorable comments he actually made." Even so, Ruppelt saw with perfect vision the fatal weakness of the skeptical case, writing early in *Report*, "There is a certain mathematical probability that any one of the ... speculative [prosaic] answers is correct — correct for this one case. If you try this type of speculation on hundreds of sightings with 'unknown' answers, the probability that the speculative answers are correct rapidly approaches zero."

Beyond that, it must be said that as history of the early official response to the UFO phenomenon, *Report* is only a first draft. Of course, all things, including UFO histories (of which Ruppelt's book is surely the first), have to start somewhere. Through the Freedom of Information Act and researchers' interviews with retired Air Force and CIA personnel who knew Ruppelt or at least co-existed in the same world, today we have a far richer, rounded picture of the personalities, the decision making processes, the bureaucratic in-fighting, and the cases themselves. In our time no serious inquirer would read *Report* without having at immediate hand Michael David Hall and Wendy Ann Connors's *Captain Edward J. Ruppelt: Summer of the Saucers — 1952* (2000) to find out what Ruppelt didn't reveal and, in many cases, may have been only marginally aware of, or utterly oblivious to, himself.

Still, Ruppelt looms deservedly large in UFO history. *The Report* is, within its limits, candid and revelatory, and the best sightings it recounts remain as puzzling now as they were then, even if Ruppelt could never quite come to grips with their implications. And in that sense Ruppelt stands in for the world's eventual failure to come to grips with the phenomenon. It was, after all, only in 1952, in the middle of Ruppelt's tenure at Blue Book, that a respected, mass circulation mainstream magazine such as *Life* could actually ask "Have We Visitors from Space?" and answer, in effect, in the affirmative without being laughed out of existence. And it was only then that a public government UFO agency, Ruppelt's Blue Book, could conduct a largely open-minded, even-handed inquiry, one that reached a telling conclusion which still seems true — that after proper investigation between twenty and thirty per cent of ostensible UFO reports will remain unexplained — even if Blue Book after Ruppelt did all in its power to make that seem not true, knowing perfectly well what that finding means if true. As we look back, the UFO phenomenon of 1952, and the Air Force project that tried to take it on, resemble nothing so much as a lost world, a legend, a myth, a golden age. It is hard to believe it ever existed.

Good soldier that he was, as bright and energetic as he was unimaginative, Ruppelt did his job well and ended up telling us more than we knew, and himself more than he wanted to know. He was blind then in the way that most of us have made ourselves blind ever since. In the brilliant recreation of Ruppelt's mental universe that you are about to read, Colin Bennett expresses it as cogently as I have seen anywhere:

> Since the conclusion of the Air Force was that UFOs posed no threat to the United States, this put the people of the United States in a very peculiar position. Let us suppose that when a family sits down for dinner each night, quite often, a man walks through the dining room and disappears through a wall. Since this man shows no interest in or violent intention towards the family, they eat in peace and take no notice. Thus do they manage the event and integrate the utterly fantastic into the mundane scheme, even though the event is acausal. They make the man and his actions invisible by reprogramming their cognitive responses, knowing full well that this liminal event had no connection with known economic or social schema. The single consideration of the absence of violence is the key to what is seen, recognized, and interpreted, and what is not. The need to ask about the quantitative and qualitative structure, the nature and characteristics of the event, is obliterated as if by a surgical operation.

If it was not a threat, to Ruppelt, his associates, and his generation it was finally irrelevant, and if it was irrelevant, it finally had no claim to being a question in any context. Toward the end of his life, Ruppelt was gathering material for a book on the history of domestic air service. Had he lived to write it, we may safely assume, I think, that it would now be long forgotten. But the ghost Ruppelt helped raise, in spite of himself, still walks through the dining room.

Jerome Clark
Canby, Minnesota
September 3, 2003

Prologue

UP TO HIS APPOINTMENT AS HEAD OF THE USAF PROJECT Blue Book in 1951, there had hardly been a single moment of Edward Ruppelt's adult life in which he was not vitally involved with aircraft and flying in some aspect or other, both in peace and war, and civilian and military life. He was thus an American who inherited in every sense all the magical traditions of flight, though he was a man who would hardly have called it such. But no military world is ever the very best environment for the kind of out-of-the-box speculation required by UFO studies. In all fairness to our brave Captain, it could be said that not being any kind of philosopher, he was given a task that would have daunted the very mightiest of philosophers.

It is likely that Ruppelt put his phenomenal energy into Blue Book because in every sense this Project represented his second youth, the War having taken his first. *The Report on Unidentified Flying Objects* shows that as distinct from almost all others around him, he is still growing, still asking questions, still up on his feet and moving. Not surprisingly, given this infusion of new energies in his second chance at a kind of youth, on occasion he hesitates: frequently, he goes for the interplanetary solution to the UFO phenomenon, only to fall short of a definite statement; often his concentration fails; he shrugs his shoulders, worried by his own daring, perhaps. Like most American heroes, he has something of Melville's Captain Ahab in him. Like Ahab, Ruppelt knows that no man was ever built for this level of endeavour, but nevertheless there is something in him that tries again and again to capture the white whale of the UFO. Though he still has a growing mind, he feels often that he isn't big enough for the task. Yet still he grows. Yet still he feels, as if looking down from a great height, that he isn't big enough. But his genes will not let him go. There is pure sky and pure airplane in him, and neither will release him from his American enchantment, born on December 17, 1903, when the Wright Flyer took off from Kitty Hawk. Like two other American visionaries of the twentieth century, George Adamski and Charles Fort, Ruppelt has the landscapes of Captain Ahab's impossibilities in him, perhaps with a touch of the dying fall of Hemingway's inspired despair. Admittedly Ruppelt was not born or built on this psychic scale, but the forces of destiny rarely take account of human scale. That he wrote a book at all puts him head and shoulders above far more clever men who chose to write nothing at all. He found himself to be a writer of more than worthy prose, and his *Report on Unidentified Flying Objects* can be put on the shelf with the books of other great twentieth century warriors, such as Che Guevara's *Reminiscences of the Cuban Revolutionary War,* and T.E. Lawrence's *Seven Pillars of Wisdom.*

AS THE AUTHOR OF TWO biographies of American writers, I know that looking for the heart of a human being is like looking for Bigfoot or indeed the UFO itself. The only way of taking such an up-river journey is to work in images and atmospheres, and as that great novelist Toni Morrison said, let the trail talk to you in its own way and in its own good time. Those great Easter Island gods that researchers call "mechanical facts," are often piled on top of one another to infinity and equated to the "truth" of the school room map. I do not intend counting such infinite sand grains of Kafka's castle and writing a book sufficient to make warthogs roll over and die, squint eyed with grief. Such writers end up like old chained bears in failing zoos; their heads go from side to side in a kind of factual dementia, an affliction of archivists, skeptics, doomed rationalists, and borough librarians.

Therefore dear readers please do not expect this book to be a model of good behaviour, if only because not a single writer worth a piece of bread pudding ever behaves correctly. If they do, let us all be profoundly suspicious of what they say. In this respect I do all the wrong things. Like someone indeed searching for the UFO, I end up blind alleys; I ignore the obvious; I dream, guess, make mistakes, and ignore or reject all sensible easy and safe solutions, as deceptive sirens leading me away from where I want to go. I deceive myself, I get utterly lost, I fight my way through that scandalous set of old frauds that garage minds call the Real (that great mandarin impostor above all other impostors), until one day a little of the code is broken and the blushing Real breaks like a seed pod and pours forth scandalous agendas and conspiracies and plots and images like a gone-mad Las Vegas fruit machine. Yes, it is a hard way of doing it. But all these seeds form questions in themselves, flying to and fro in the heads of authors like Shakespeare's Ariel. Bits and pieces of the human puzzle speaking old languages rediscovered come to lead an author out to the

13

initiations of time and personality.

That magic bird of American youth which flew from its alchemical flask on December 17, 1903, at Kitty Hawk, North Carolina, was the first great American escape of the twentieth century. No other nation smothered by mass arrests, social control, and endless slaughter practiced by the two socialisms could have created such an image of breakout through flight. No other nation had the nerve and imagination to give birth to such an impossible vehicle, built of all dreams of all magical escapes. This act of first flight denied that life was for punishment, work, suffering, incarceration, and little else. The Wright Brothers' *Flyer* broke the mundane cast of lingering Victorian life forever. In this sense America invented happiness, enjoyment and pleasure, things almost absent from human history, and America has never been forgiven for it. In creating flight it gave birth to all notions of twentieth century possibilities of transcendence, of both flesh and mind. The rocket, space station, and shuttle have never ceased being inspiring metaphors for courage, danger, romance and genius.

RUPPELT LOOKED UPON his task of investigating the flying saucer phenomenon as essentially a somewhat technological one. Good books about technology and society are most rare. The masterly achievements of Norman Mailer in *A Fire on the Moon* and Tom Wolfe in *The Right Stuff* are but two of a mere handful of possible examples. Generally speaking, the great root cultures of the Western World, be they Arts, Literature or Philosophy, have ignored technology if only because it sprang from the alleys of the early Industrial Revolution, and not from the Universities. Technology, at least in the older societies, was hence somewhat communistic, proletarian; it sprang from dirty hands and equally dirty plotting minds. It hissed and stank, laid waste to the environment, and it created vulgar New Money. More importantly, technology as a new culture had no fashionable grand aesthetic style in any sense that the early twentieth century understood.

But the unforgivable sin of technology was that it demanded brain, and brain in those far off days was still as bad a word as ever it was, as far as traditional social mores went. Even at Balliol over a half century later, only those brains were praised that looked backwards in time: brains concerned with aspects of burgeoning ultra modernism were looked upon with that suspicion of swarthy foreigners way beyond Calais. In this respect I spread terror. I mentioned cybernetics and computers one day to two friendly dons, both world famous. Quite alarmed, they fled to a safer part of the main quad, for all the world like twilight stick-figures sketched by Max Beerbohm for an age of Hansom cabs.

In America brains and technology had a chance, but in Britain, despite the Industrial Revolution, such things were still locked away in the west wing like a mad relative or a malformed child born without benefit of clergy. This British urge to self destruction was profound. Should anyone doubt this, they should remember the ritual crucifixion by the Establishment of Alan Turing,[1] the genius who created the first digital computer, and the destruction of the TSR2, certainly one of the great warplanes of all time. It was destroyed on the order of certain Labour government ministers who should have been arrested and charged with espionage.

During the eighteen months of Ruppelt's tenure as head of Project Blue Book, all appeared to be well with America, despite the Korean War; even the dour military industrial complex was young, and indeed was not much of a Complex as yet. Massive faceless corporate bureaucracy had arrived indeed, but it still had lands to conquer, and whilst investigating UFO sightings, Ruppelt travelled around American laboratories, airfields and military bases. Either in or out of uniform, he was free to drop in any time, anywhere to workshops, factories, laboratories, research institutions, universities, and top secret nuclear installations such as Los Alamos,[2] Oak Ridge,[3] and the Hanford plant,[4] places of which the UFOs were particularly fond.[5]

A US Air Force officer of the present day in an equivalent capacity could do no such thing. In the early 1950s there was still a kind of family atmosphere in the American armed forces, an atmosphere now as vanished as late Rome. The airplanes themselves were big silver friendly things, almost like friendly toys with a smile on their face; they could be made into pots and pans and cars when they died a decent death. They didn't look as if they hated you, they were not black or camouflaged; they didn't look like spiteful bat-like things to be burned in toxic pits with a stake through their heart, and they did not have disturbing names like Stealth.

The military arm was still properly socialized. Apart from munitions areas, many US air bases were unfenced, and scouts and guides, spotting clubs, and enthusiasts of all kinds could walk by the flight lines. At weekends, dad could place junior and the family by the cockpit of a fighter and take a snapshot. The American people belonged to this integrated structure; generations of families worked in it, and were proud of what they did.

Factory hooters still sounded, and hordes of workers with their own tool and lunchboxes would surge to canteens and main gates where there were very few guards. National threats were finite, external;

they were still describable in plain terms. Like America's aircraft, they had a name and a face. Today's complicated threats, some internal, others shape-shifting and yet others indefinable (such as Y2K, 9/11, viral combats, information wars, and social control through a culture of advertisements, entertainment and media) had not yet arrived in the American consciousness in the modern sense.

Yes, the aircraft and the new consumer products (which they resembled somewhat) were mostly big and visible things, and a good mechanic could still understand the processes involved in their design, manufacture and operation. Masses of drooping wiring were still extant, together with point-to-point soldered connections. Industrial reality was still a flow diagram — yes, getting bigger and more complex, but its stages in relation to one another could nevertheless be understood as a whole. What was more important is that they could be seen as being processes linked to hand and brain and hence to family and society. The computer chip had not yet arrived to demolish utterly the common visible social processes of the past. Similarly, workers were not yet taken to work in curtained buses to places like Area 51, where they made things that appeared to have no connection with any other thing in any significant sense.

By comparison, Ruppelt's world could be measured and predicted. Names, prices, addresses, and complete social identities had not yet vanished into twenty-digit numbers and barcodes. But what the philosopher Hobbes called the Leviathan, that is the living body of mind, mechanism and society, was being changed utterly, becoming more complicated by the techno-consumer hour. Ruppelt had probably not heard of Hobbes, yet some threat of loss of a future identity was present in his make up. In one sense, *The Report on Unidentified Flying Objects* is a learning process through which Ruppelt comes to recognize that the world he lives and works in is becoming rapidly a far more complicated place than he ever conceived it to be.

Considering the mission Ruppelt undertook, the Air Force was sparing on expenses. Since he was forced to use bus stops, trains and taxis as if he were as much importance to the Air Force as a travelling canteen salesman, he eventually grew somewhat bitter. But his pleasant nature certainly opened a lot of doors, as did his good looks and his charm. He was welcomed by well-known faces of the military and scientific culture as readily as if he were dropping in to the local diner. Vertical access was equally as easy, and Generals were to be found in oil stained overalls alongside besuited scientists and harassed designers. For this last brief time of its initial fertilization, the military industrial complex had faces and names. There were nationally known characters around such as Chuck Yeager, Ed Heinemann of Douglas Aircraft (designer of the *Dauntless* and the A-4 *Skyhawk*), and Bill Allen of Boeing (designer of the B-52, then called the *Stratofortress*), and of course Curtis LeMay and General MacArthur. The great flying ace Lindbergh was of course still very much alive and well, but his status as American Hero was somewhat marred by this time due to his political views. User-friendly family firms with mythological names were still branded on the American soul: Curtis-Wright, Langley, Chance-Vaught, Northrop, Convair, Bell, Lockheed. We must include of course IBM who, at this time, before the transistor arrived, were forever struggling with the problem of how to get computers small enough to put into missiles and aircraft.

A half century later, it is difficult for the public to give names and faces to the bland anonymous processes that have replaced this lost pantheon of names of old projects, experiments, and military-industrial developments. Ever since the Condon Committee[6] of 1968, which overlapped the issues of both of Watergate and Vietnam, the US military has been less than enthusiastic as regards the asking of fundamental questions, and certainly the type of Air Force officer who had Ruppelt's good natured freedom to talk to whoever he liked about whatever he liked, does not now exist. Unfortunately, the terrible events of 9/11 have served to make things far worse in this respect.

But even during this time of relative innocence, the military-scientific culture was preparing to conceal itself, to cut itself off from society in the tradition of what General Groves of Los Alamos called "Big Science." In Ruppelt's time this process of monkish concealment was just beginning. Though America appears to be growing in all and every direction technologically (as it still is), socially it is in decline. We thus have two rhythms that Gibbon saw in late Rome: hot house growth for a specialized elite, and military adventures, accompanied by slow but inexorable social decay.

Ruppelt therefore inhabits a dream city in which he walks down the centre thoroughfare and see blinds being drawn, doors secured and windows being boarded up, at the same time as he sees the growth of all kinds of New Town on the horizon. This strange landscape is the subtext to his experience. He sees this hidden UFO country almost as a thing temporarily imposed upon received reality, only to fade away quickly as normality returns. But despite himself, Ruppelt is disturbed by what he has seen and heard; fragments of these possibilities remain with him. The UFO experience to any degree has this universal effect. The house of the mind is turned upside down, and the furniture cannot be put back exactly into place again.

We have here a drama between men and systems whose story trails back to Huxley's *Brave New World*, Orwell's *1984*, the novels of Kafka, and indeed right back to Shakespeare's worldview.

WHEN EDWARD RUPPELT joined 677 squadron 444th Bomb Group of the 20th Air Force on December 14, 1944, he became part of a technological systems animal. As if he were not already become part of its blood and bones, he served to extend further the ambitions, dreams and destinies of the larger scale of being of the Air Force, where ancestors, systems, and men and women formed part of a unique twentieth century cosmos.

In that flying was in his blood, Ruppelt's psychic inheritance was as fabulous a mythology as the Egyptian Book of the Dead, or the demonological lists of *The Malleus Maleficarum*. The young man from Iowa entered a highly developed part of an historical process of selecting and rejecting numberless analogies of bird flight, men's muscular power, and of course the sea. The old prints and books show attempts at flight, up-in-the-air go boats, oars, keels and sails.[7] In carts, boats, coaches, and hay-barn constructions, the crews take off their hats to sun, moon and the gods of the four winds as they float through storm and cloud in beautifully impossible contraptions. The lack of suitable engines did not deter these well dressed heroes. Many stuck heavy steam engines inside fairy tale structures and crossed their fingers. Others preferred balloons, hand-pumped propellers, and disastrous early parachutes. Yet others were happy to sketch tethered eagles hoisting wood and steel battleships, their decks loaded with heavy cannon and stores. Other designs show tent-like structures soaring through the cosmos with entire families aboard; rowing boats with moth-like wings are supported by squadrons of birds; half-naked men and women are borne aloft by huge air-filled pumpkins complete with crow's nests and sails, anchors, and smoking chimneys. In early sketches of possible flight, men are fired to the moon inside shell-like projectiles; farm carts are borne aloft by gasbags, which take men and women on tours of planets rich in forests, rivers and animals.

Looking back at the playful phantasmagoria that is the history of flight, it can be seen that modern technical conceptions had a magical birth. The first moment of powered flight at Kitty Hawk is constructed of all the moments of nonsense that went before. Such is the nature of that complex imposture called technological time. We may be forced to accept that nonsense games are as much at the heart of cultural formation as are the input/output socio-economic games of the traditional historical view.

18

Therefore rather like Francis Bacon (and indeed Chaucer before him), Ruppelt stood with one foot in the old cosmos and the other firmly planted in the new. History will view the twenty years after 1945 as being rather like the early seventeenth century; that is a going from one world to another in a time between the ending of the great Renaissance era and the first phases of the so-called Enlightenment. In the world of Ruppelt's second youth after 1945, media for example, had hardly arrived in the modern sense. Objectivity and fact were still around, the world was still a solid place; the brain was a Pavlovian computer, a behaviorist mass of hard wiring that processed information in a suspiciously orderly way. There were still definable inputs and outputs in a world in which appearances still had moral and material value; teachers taught, scientists discovered, doctors cured, governments made policies, and the armed forces and police protected the nation. The conspiracies and mysteries of the major American assassinations alone (never mind the UFO) were to shake the foundations of this cartoon world, whose fairy tales came to be seen as quite understandable protective screens, rather like the "solid truths" of a passing Victorian world, truths which were rank with any and every kind of decay.

But techno-industrial time runs fast. Wilbur Wright and Lindbergh were still alive, but Ruppelt's generation regarded their world as Chaucer looked upon knights in armour, holy relics and countless fragments of the True Cross.

In the onrush of media time, the real and the unreal were to disappear somewhere between the first flickering black and white TV sets and the World Wide Web. Ruppelt felt the first edge of this indeterminate world and in his UFO investigations, as we shall see, at times he glanced from one to another and didn't quite know what to do.

The Report on Unidentified Flying Objects is therefore an essay not so much about how we seek those crude divisions between falsehood and truth beloved by sceptics, but how wonder and fear, technology and inspiration, were *managed* in a cosmos that was beginning to change more rapidly than perhaps any cosmos had ever changed. The differentials between bewildering states of what was, what had been, and what was to come, created a world of high contrast relief, full of the drama and intense colour of a Dalí painting, brimming with profligate growth amidst shadows, nervous expectations, and plain fear. To make matters worse as far as the military were concerned, the "flying saucer," as it was then known, smelt of the esoteric. Military men hated the esoteric more than all other enemies in a world that was getting a little too complicated for the traditional military person.

For a man thrown headfirst from his task of examining the innards of the Russian Mig-15 fighter into something only partly measurable in human and scientific terms, Ruppelt writes of the UFO phenomenon with great clarity and ease. There is humour, drama, and much atmosphere in *The Report on Unidentified Flying Objects*. His brisk, informative style gives dates, places, and he threads in much easily assimilated technical information as the censorship of the time allowed. He has also a respect for his subject: he conveys a sense of awe and mystery in plain terms, not an easy thing to do. Thus, though his book appears to be the history of a practical military investigation, it is also the history of a man and his fears, doubts, and uncertainties in the knowledge that if any one of the incidents investigated by him is to any extent true, then the human race is not alone in the universe. Just one swallow in the form of the UFO makes for all possible summers.

Ruppelt meets scared policemen, frightened housewives, and pale-faced pilots straight out of the cockpit, dragging their parachutes. Often their mental state is that of fish thrown back into the water with a fine tale to tell. These tales all form a growing delta mouth of stories in Ruppelt's mind: some have measurable scientific dimensions, others are truly fantastic. On the very fringe of the UFO horizon, there are the rejected stories, the accounts of abductions and meetings with aliens. Hans Christian Andersen and the Brothers Grimm would have loved it all. But neither before nor since has an officer of the United States Air Force had such a brief. Most of these stories are sculpted by experience and observation of unidentified flying objects that appear to be intelligently controlled; they are aware of pursuers, they are registered by radar and theodolite, and are seen by independent observers of every human condition, status, race and country.

The verification of any single one of these sightings as "not of this Earth" (or not of this culture) would have the most profound effect on humanity, as profound indeed as our own culture has had on other "inferior" cultures.

This somewhat important investigative task was given to an enlisted Air Force officer who had to stand at bus stops to get from one air base to another. We see Ruppelt and his generation therefore as figures in a landscape of a new American dawn. He might have been painted surrounded not by angels or religious symbols, but by the devotional texts and icons of the first consumer revelations of the twentieth century. The angels of Giotto are now become circuit diagrams, spare parts manuals, timetables and agendas, radar screens, lasers, dish-aerials. A demonology of speed, input and output, efficiency and fact, evidence and objectivity, all have found new flesh in the workshop and the laboratory as well as the Cash'n'Carry, the drive-in supermart and *Pig'n'Chicken Dunk'n'Dine*.

Thus after 1945 did the old world die and the new world enter a state of bewildering and perplexing growth. There was therefore in young America an atmosphere rather like that Johan Huizinga describes in *The Waning of the Middle Ages*:[8] elation, yet a quick tendency to high emotion as the cultural landscape was cleared for the supreme victory of American technology over religion, class structures, and the metaphysics of the old world. The Communists, with their felt boots, universal prison camps, and Neanderthal women who sang about their tractors were going nowhere in history. Mankind could be a chrome Cadillac success, and synthetic happiness grown as a TV Soya crop nurtured by images, advertisements, and suggestions. This was the thin end of the wedge that was to become the Virtual World of that Entertainment State in which most people now live.

Edward Ruppelt did not live to see the fall from this brief period of innocence and grace. For his brief time in history, tragedy could be avoided, or at least engineered around. Fear, that thing of which all gods are made, could at least be held back by systems analysis.

Such divine madness of America was still left unsullied within him when he died of a heart attack in 1960 at the early age of thirty five. He struggled with that American demon called the UFO and he left behind unique and definitive fragments of mid-twentieth century experience.

An American Demonology is the story of the flesh and blood of the prototype systems-man that was Edward Ruppelt. No one was born more American than he. The demons were all around him in the aircraft and the weaponry. He had all the sacred courage of the Wright Brothers and the madness of the astronauts. As thanks for this, after he died, almost every copy of his book disappeared from bookstores worldwide, never to be seen again, and they were not bought by customers. Since with the exception of Hall and Connors' excellent book *Summer of the Saucers*, neither history nor the United States Air Force gave him a memorial, I offer this book to his memory and may the gods bless forever his great American soul.

A Chain of Being

The Cosmos of the Military Industrial Complex

No American Graffiti for the Navigator

JUST AFTER MIDDAY OF AUGUST 14, 1945, ON A BEARING exactly 28.35N, 137.37E, high above the Pacific, the young bombardier/navigator of a B-29 Superfortress received a radio signal telling him that the War against Japan was over, and that the Emperor had surrendered. The plane was part of the 444th Bomb Group of United States Army Air Force and it was heading back to Tinian, the main island base in the Marianas group, after almost completely destroying Hikari Naval Base at Tokuyama, Japan. The man who received the historic signal aboard the plane was 1st Lieutenant Edward J. Ruppelt, a young man from Iowa. As one of the lead navigators, he was to receive an Oak Leaf Cluster to his DFC for leading his group to Tokuyama.

It had been a significant and exciting two weeks for Ruppelt and his crew, and indeed for all human history. For some months the men of the 58th Bombardment Wing, 20th Air Force based on the Pacific island of Tinian, must have heard excited mysterious whispers about specially equipped aircraft and new bombs of unprecedented power. A week prior to the last conventional raid on Japan, on August 6, at 8.15 am something peculiar had happened over Hiroshima. In the first milli-second after 8.16 am "a pin-prick of purplish-red light expanded to a glowing fireball hundreds of feet wide. The temperature at its core was 50,000,000°."[1] The raid on Nagasaki followed on August 9.

As Ruppelt's crew landed on Tinian, and prepared for celebration, they might well have glimpsed Enola Gay and Boxcar, the two B-29s that dropped the Hiroshima and Nagasaki bombs respectively. He might well have toasted the end of WWII in the Pacific with Colonel Paul W. Tibbets and the crew of Enola Gay. Indeed, as a lead navigator, given sudden illness or accident, Ruppelt might well have been quickly selected to put Hiroshima or Nagasaki under the cross hairs of his Norden bombsight. He must have known the faces and names of Tibbets' crew well, and indeed in all probability he could have seen a man on a tall ladder painting the words Enola Gay (the name of Tibbets' mother) over the name Great Artiste a few hours before Tibbets' plane took off on the first nuclear mission.

When a man looks back and realises that a single wounding, death, accident or illness amongst personnel could have seen him guiding a B-29 to Hiroshima with a super-weapon aboard, he never forgets such a hair-raising brush with destiny. But writing home, Ruppelt was as unrevealing as are most warriors. He played the role of the simple-minded jolly lad, quite justifiably covering up any mental scars caused by playing a part in apocalyptic destruction, or by the memory of the vast hosts of the American dead from the Pacific War. His local newspaper quoted him on the last raid of the War, saying exactly what he was expected to say: "Everything was set up perfectly," spoke Lt. Ruppelt. "The bomb run was the best I ever saw — good check points and above all we found the target open with the weather clear as a bell. It was a good mission to end everything and we're all proud of the record achieved."[2]

It had been a long war for the young man flying back to Tinian and looking forward to civilian life again. His crew-cut features are that of some long forgotten rock star, found years later perhaps under a damp pile of old 78s of Gene Vincent and Pat Boone. But there was to be no *American Graffiti* youth for young Ruppelt. He was plunged into the last two years of WWII before he even had time to breathe freely the proper air of youth. After just a semester (twelve weeks) at Iowa State Teacher's College, he went on to study Mechanical Engineering at Iowa State College, financially supported by a grant made by the G.I. Bill. Working with his sister Liz, he supported himself during the summer by running a "little general store in Yellowstone."

He joined the United States Army Air Force in 1943. After six months' training he got his wings as a bombardier/navigator, and became a 1st Lieutenant in the 677th Squadron, 444th Bomb Group, 58th Bomber Wing of the 20th Air Force. This Wing was equipped with the B-29, which then was certainly the most advanced four-engine bomber flying.

Ruppelt was almost born in this particular type of aircraft. With no youth to speak of that was not overshadowed by war, the stream-lined B-29 Superfortress must have served as a kind of nourishing surrogate mother. Designed by the Boeing Team for Pacific strategic bombing requirements, the B-29 was certainly quite a spectacular new air weapon, way ahead of its time in many respects, and compared to the previous B-17, it looked like a gleaming rocket-shape yearn-ing for outer space. Breaking all range, speed and operational height records for the time, the B-29 was the first truly systems aeroplane with fully integrated elements, including remote controlled guns and pressurization. By comparison, the lumbering and unpressurised Brit-ish Lancaster, bless its soul, had lash-up wiring, and an interior full of add-on afterthoughts. It looked like a stone-age thing by comparison with the B-29 (which did not serve in Europe), but nevertheless, the Lancaster was good enough to play a major role in destroying the industry of Nazi Germany.

The B-29 was rushed into production and placed in the hands of airmen months before it should have been, and the airmen and ground crews were left to cope for themselves. The first machines off the production line suffered explosive decompression at altitude, engine temperatures soaring above 300°C, props that refused to "feather," remote controlled turrets "cooking off" and spraying .50 cal bullets into the formation, and the airframe suffered multiple stresses from unprecedented loading. In India there were cooling problems, resulting in many engine fires, perhaps consuming a wing before men could bail out, and gunners "cannon balled" out of the aircraft when the pres-sure seals failed on their blister canopies. Many times Ruppelt must have wondered whether he was going to come out of the War alive, not because of Japanese action, but through systems or structural failure of his aircraft.

In nine combat missions as a bombardier/navigator based at Dudkhundi, India (and also Kwanghan, China), he flew over Siam, Manchuria, Singapore, Rangoon and Kuala Lumpur. In the spring of 1945 he was posted to Tinian, an island in the Pacific. This base was to become the main B-29 heavy bomber base, formed to provide the strategic air support for what was planned to be the future assault on the Japanese mainland.

Though he was to prove himself one of the great discursive chroniclers of twentieth century military history, Ruppelt may well have taken note that whilst this first B-29 experience in Asia was not a complete disaster, it was not a great success. This example of how big-systems technology could fail as well as succeed may have gone deeper than ever he realized at the time. This two-sided view (held by very few in the USAAF at the time), might well have influenced his later UFO investigations, where he saw, time and time again, a big system trying to focus on the UFO phenomenon and not succeeding because it did not have the kind of mental resolving power required. On a much larger scale, of course, the same thing happened in Vietnam twenty years later. Barefoot peasants with rifles passed through the interstices of the cognitive resolution of the mightiest military machine in the world and forced it off the battlefield. Like the UFO, the effective fighting power of the Vietnamese peasantry was an almost-impossibility.

Ruppelt's bombing group was part of Operation Matterhorn, which was a plan to create bases in China from where operations against the Japanese mainland could be launched. Great were the hopes that the splendid new technology of the B-29 bomber would triumph, but the ground conditions were totally unsuitable, the supply problems terribly difficult, and the bombers had to have a whole wing of fighters and their entire backup and communications committed to merely protecting their bases. Eventually all four of the B-29 groups based around Chengtu in China had to be withdrawn to Tinian, from where they were devastatingly more effective in the bombing of the Japanese mainland and in supporting the island invasions.

Such was Ruppelt's first bracing experience with the burgeoning military industrial complex and its interface with war, global politics, powerful new weapons systems and evolving technologies. Thus his wartime experience gave him access to many different landscapes, and the really interesting thing about Ruppelt is that he had the kind of brain that never ever stops working on such things, whether sleeping or waking.

He most probably didn't know it, but UFOs were not very far away from him at this time. During operations, his 444th Bomb group reported:

N — 1945.05.15 — Night, Nogoya, Japan.

B-29, 444th Bomb Group, "The first sighting of a ball of fire" was made on this mission. (444th Bombardment Group history.)

N — 1945.05.23 — Night, Tokyo, Japan.

B-29, 444th Bomb Group, "Three balls of fire" reported. (444th Bombardment Group history.)

Mig–15

AFTER HE LEFT THE AIR FORCE, Ruppelt took a job at Northrop Aviation Corporation in Los Angeles, a firm that, thanks to its founder Jack Northrop, had always been at the very cutting edge of aircraft design. After research spanning almost twenty years, Northrop Aviation produced quite revolutionary jet-powered "flying wing" designs in the immediate post-war period. These were at least the equivalent to those of the legendary Horton brothers in Nazi Germany.[3] Therefore for a young man such as Ruppelt, whose life-long interest was aircraft, Northrop was an exciting place to be at this time. He must have heard all kinds of new-technology discussions about aircraft design such as the B-35 "flying wing" jet bomber. In 1948, the fully developed B-35 design was accepted by the Air Force, and Northrop began the assembly of thirteen airframes. However, as an example of the kind of military stupidity we shall encounter many times in this book, the Air Force in its wisdom cancelled the order in preference to the Convair B-36 Peacemaker. The B-36 was just about the most ridiculous flying white elephant delivered to any air arm anywhere. However it did last for nearly eight years as a frontline strategic bomber before being replaced by the B-52, a design which is still in full combat service fifty years after the first prototype flew in.[4]

Just like the British TSR2, the Northrop B-35 flying wing would have had a possible forty year life, steadily mutating into the Stealth B-2 Spirit bomber generations later. But as we shall see, as soon as the limited military mind overrules the scientific and civilian sector, there is nearly always a disaster waiting to happen.

The B-36 was very much Air Force General Curtis LeMay's baby, and it became the starship of the Strategic Air Command. This impressive looking bomber appears quite a few times in Ruppelt's *The Report on Unidentified Flying Objects* because in the 1950s, for better or for worse, it became for a short while the main strategic bombing aircraft of the Air Force, though its general performance was somewhat modest. Also, its development potential compared with the Flying Wing was very limited, its multi-engine (jet and prop) configuration showing beyond doubt that the designers of the B-36 were in an uncertain change-over period as far as aircraft power plants were concerned. In any case, despite LeMay's powerful claims, it is extremely doubtful if this bomber would ever have survived a Mig-15 fighter screen on a deep penetration mission. The only thing the B-36 had to offer was an unforgettable sight and sound, particularly at night. For these reasons, it was readily used by Air Force Intelligence officers in particular as a culprit for UFO sightings, even though often it was later verified that no B-36 was in the air at the time of the sighting.

Between 1945 and 1950, being fully absorbed in Northrop matters as he was, Ruppelt might yet again have taken full note of the B-36 affair as an example of yet another big systems failure involving the young military industrial complex. But our hero had a lot on his plate. He became a navigator in the Reserve 89th troop transport wing, based at Offutt AFB in Nebraska, and at the same time he worked his way through an aeronautical degree at Iowa State College.

He was recalled to active duty status because of the outbreak of the Korean War. On January 4, 1951, he left Offutt AFB and the following day became part of 1125th Field Activities Group at Wright Patterson AFB at Dayton, Ohio. This Group was an Intelligence unit, and Ruppelt was assigned to Air Technical Intelligence 26, which became known as the more familiar Air Technical Intelligence Command — or ATIC — very soon after Ruppelt resumed his duty.

Within ATIC, his first job was to help with a performance-analysis of the Soviet Union's Mig-15 jet fighter.[5] In the workshops and test laboratories of Wright Patterson AFB, every available piece of scrap from Mig-15 aircraft, either crashed, shot down or captured, was closely examined. Though the Cold War was at its height, nevertheless relevant documents from a thousand and one sources in Europe and Asia flooded into ATIC, some of them bloodstained. In this work Ruppelt was more an executive organizer than analyst; he helped integrate the mass of different kinds of information gleaned by specialists from propulsion units, airframe, electronics, and weaponry into a whole picture, with clear working handbooks and drawings. These were to assist in an overall comparison by ATIC of Soviet Union manufacturing, construction, design and tactical concepts. This information enabled specialists to make comparisons with current American aeronautical and general industrial practice. It also helped them to use good Russo-German ideas without benefit of clergy, so to speak.

Although basically derived from a Fock Wulfe design by Kurt Tank, the lumpy Mig-15 was quite an achievement, and came as something of a surprise to the West. The aircraft itself was Communism personified, and it was thus something of a political airplane. It needed no highly specialized pilot skills or long, vulnerable runways, and it looked as if it had been assembled in a field by peasant garage-hands. But like the Vietnamese (and Vietminh) peasant battalions, again it was a winner, and as such was a cause of intense embarrassment to the proud Western military-industrial ego. It was a cheap aircraft to produce, and was of simple practicality and strength. Over a thirty year span, like the various versions of the war-winning T-34 tank,[6] the Mig-15 and its variants were handed over in many thousands to Communist satellite countries. The machine was Communist again in that its engine was an unlicensed and unblushing copy of the Rolls Royce Nene engine, some samples of which had been obligingly handed to the Russians on a plate, probably by British fellow travellers, plenty of whom were active in both Britain and America at this time, witness the Russian theft of atomic bomb secrets from both countries.

It showed certainly that the Russians, by hook or by crook, were more than capable of producing world-beating weaponry.

The famous Soviet fighter examined by Ruppelt was not a very handsome machine compared to the lines of the pretty and petite North American F-86A Sabre, but it was a hell of a dogfighter. The 6,000 lb. thrust of the early Mig-15 models gave a considerable climb-and-turn advantage over the 3,750 lbs thrust of the Sabre's Allison J35-C-3 turbojet, for example. The influence of German excellent wartime design practice, inside and out, was evident also. The back of the fuselage came off complete, and the engine could be removed by four men in one hour, which was a damn sight better than US air maintenance crews could do with the J35 engine of the Sabre, which was an unholy lash-up of pipes, awkward stanchions, wiring cables and fuel lines.

The nose-weapon pack of the MiG included an impressive 37mm cannon, and this must also have interested Ruppelt. This pack was a superbly engineered retractable modular unit, again somewhat German in inspiration. Extremely neat and compact, the whole pod could be quickly hand-cranked down from the nose of the Mig for rapid maintenance and rearmament. By comparison the .50 cal machine guns of the F86 Sabre were inadequate in Korean combat.

All in all, the Mig-15 was as much of a shock technologically as were the German V-weapons and Messerschmitt 262 jet fighter of 1944–45. From its superb undercarriage mechanics to its cockpit display, from its general finish and aerodynamic design, it was a state of the art airplane. It had another aspect that would certainly have interested Ruppelt. It was a concept design, a true systems-airplane, and its engineering compared well with the techniques used by prototype B-47 and B-52 jet bombers, both flying fully operationally within Ruppelt's unfortunately short lifetime. It could be said that the appearance of such aircraft as the Mig-15 started a technological paranoia that reached a peak with the bleep-bleep of Sputnik 1, on October 4, 1957, and gave a hurried birth to the space race.

The Mig had also impressive miniature electronics for its time. These were almost certainly East German in origin. Its acorn sized "Gnom" type vacuum tubes clipped firmly into snug bases and these were soldered to modular printed circuit boards, each of which had a clearly defined function, as is the modern practice. These thin, lightweight boards (made of the Russian equivalent to Paxolin, an inert pre-plastic fibrous material) were connected by minimal-path cable layout and integrated plug-and-socket harnessing. This suggested strongly that a lot of this fine equipment was designed by press-ganged meticulous German experts. The internal layout of electronics, hydraulics and electrical control equipment mirrored the immaculate high-standard layouts of such late German advanced jets as the Me 262b-1, a two seat radar equipped night fighter, and the jet bomber Arado 234b. Examples of these aircraft were brought to ATIC after the War, along with the bat-winged Horton brothers' Ho IX V3. This twin-jet fighter, an almost science fiction design for fifty years ago, was certainly the inspiration for the B-2 Spirit "Stealth" bomber which, apart from size, it resembles almost completely. The intriguing carcass of the Ho IX V3 is now on display in the National Air and Space Museum. Those readers who wish to follow the Stealth developments beyond the scope of this book might like to read the *The F117 Story* in Combat Diary 22.[7]

Other than the bits and pieces from Korea, much information on the Mig-15 comes from countries under the Soviet Occupation. A lot of equipment for this aircraft was manufactured at the Pirna plant in East Germany, and great risks were taken by Western sympathisers to get out technical intelligence under the noses of the Russians. Manfred Gerlach was the technical manager of the Pirna aircraft plant, and he travelled to Darmstadt (in the Western Zone) bringing out six hundred microfilms of technical drawings and photographs. Eventually, he was caught and sentenced to life imprisonment by the East Germans.

In 1951, ATIC also received much high quality intelligence of a similar nature from Hans Held, who was supervisor of the Junkers Aircraft Works at Dessau at this time. Another man, one Rudert, who held a managerial post at the VEB electrical factory at Efurt, also contributed much of value to ATIC. He produced information and drawings of the then new "Gnom" vacuum tubes. Both Held and Rudert were sentenced to death by the Supreme Court of the German Democratic Republic on January 7, 1956.

All these men worked for Reinhardt Gehlen,[8] the ex-Nazi Intelligence Chief who was later put in power as a spy chief in West Germany by Alan Dulles.[9]

Practically all such relevant air-technical information from Europe (and Korea) finally finished up on the desk of Lieutenant Colonel Rosengarten at Wright Patterson Air Force Base at Dayton, Ohio. Rosengarten was Head of the Performance and Characteristics Branch, which came under the Aircraft and Propulsion Section within the ATIC Analysis Division. In turn, Rosengarten funnelled most of the Mig-15 information direct to Ruppelt, who was one of the very few men at ATIC properly qualified to assess and interpret the flow of information. Rosengarten's departmental responsibilities also included Project Grudge, an almost redundant UFO research department that was all that was left of a number of abandoned Air Force UFO investigation projects, all of which were victims of neglect, cost-cutting, prejudice and often plain ignorance and blindness.

Rosengarten was a clever and much-admired man. He was an officer who knew how to handle men and projects within what researchers Hall and Connors have revealed to be often an abrasive environment full of egos and minimal expense accounts, incompetents, and mental laziness as well as good men and true.

Project Grudge was certainly not going to get out of the doldrums whilst the Head of ATIC was the formidable Colonel (later Brigadier-General) Harold Watson,[10] who was 100 per cent anti-saucer, as were quite a few of his staff. Although others under him (such as Rosengarten) were far less negative, they kept their ideas very much to themselves when Watson was around, only opening up to Ruppelt in private conversations.

Watson, who was chief of ATIC between 1949 and 1951, was a hard man, very much a brilliant flier of the old school. His good looks and blond hair were straight from a John Wayne movie, but though he possessed a Masters Degree in Aeronautical Engineering, he was strictly negative as far as things such as UFOs were concerned. He was a fabled wartime fighter ace, but as with most great warriors, he was not a man of high intellect and imagination.

Nevertheless, Watson was highly regarded in the Air Force. As one of the leading lights in the very earliest phase of American jet fighter development, Watson had flight-tested the revolutionary German Me 262 jet fighter, the most advanced jet fighter in the world at that time.[11] He was instrumental also in shipping samples of any and every kind of German equipment to ATIC for detailed examination, including some Horton models. He worked closely with the UFO-neutral Rosengarten, who played a large part of the concept-development of the P-80 Shooting Star, which was the first operational jet fighter in what was soon to become the independent

United States Air Force. Many of the features of the Me 262 were built into the P-80, but unfortunately, though a fine aircraft, the P-80 did not have anything like the looks and lines of the wickedly beautiful Me 262. Since little was known about swept-back wings, the P-80 was given a pair of straight wings, which showed how hesitant was some American design thinking at the time compared to German practise. Nevertheless, the P-80 flew forty per cent of the fighter missions in Korea,[12] and was the first Western jet fighter to meet the Mig-15s and indeed shoot down quite of a few of them — though through superior pilot skill and good training more than anything else.

Nothing better shows Watson's attitude to UFOs than International News Service reporter Bob Considine's interview with him in November 1950. Watson claimed, "At the end of nearly every report tracked down stands a crackpot, a religious crank, a publicity hound, or a malicious practical joker." He admitted that airline pilots were convinced that they themselves had seen something quite extraordinary, but he attributed these sightings to such things as fatigue and windshield reflections. The denial policy of the Air Force only served to antagonize seasoned and experienced civilian pilots of all kinds.

THIS AMOUNT OF DETAIL is included here because it gives something of the smell, taste and touch of the electro-mechanical environment of the immediate post-War world that grew through Ruppelt's being like ivy through a wall. In order to know a man we must know what he is made of, from where he draws his inspirations, dreams and energies, what gods look after him, and of what domains he is the guardian.

From Ruppelt's earliest youth, given his intense experience of the electro-mechanical worldview and his experience of very little else, this world defined him in time. Thus the idea of mechanical inputs and outputs structured all the metaphors within the values and social norms of Ruppelt's society. Moreover these ideas appeared to be at the time historically "successful" in that religion, metaphysics, occultism, all things of the spirit were in full cultural retreat before experimental mechanism and electro-bio-chemical progeny.

It was hence a complete cosmos in Tillyard's sense, in that Ruppelt's world was beginning to refer to almost every single aspect of techno-military-industrialism in terms of that much-abused concept we call "reality." In the respect that it challenged the almost self-evident assumptions of this equation, the coming of the UFO was a shock, both physically and psychically. It did not fit the output=input world of what was far too easily assumed to be "reality." Every single aspect of the

31

experience of the industrial cosmos was conceived as an output from a finite input. In Ruppelt's time, the idea of information and advertising as complex forms of virtual image-life had hardly yet arrived. Images, media and advertising were still confined largely to things seen once a year on Christmas trees. That these "new" cosmological forces were about to break out like gremlins and make vital definitions even more complicated than they were already was a thing that, for better or for worse, our hero did not live to see.

The World as Mechanism

WITH ALL HIS EXPERIENCE of electro-mechanical devices and ideas both in war and peace, and in military and civilian life, Ruppelt was now a vintage systems animal *par excellence*; he knew the theory and practice of almost every significant piece of equipment in the US Air Force at this time. At this point the Mig-15 and his mind are almost metaphorically identical: we see his brain and the culture simultaneously: hard-wired, visual, a mirror of flow diagrams with tangible inputs and outputs. Ruppelt signifies both Mind and Machine and America moving forward in History at an unprecedented pace towards the Product Cosmos in which all and everything is finite Design; even knowledge and language (if and when stripped of metaphor and all ambiguity, of course!) were both expressions of rationalized resource-development; one piece of experimentation joined to another, rather like the early science fiction view of space stations. This was analogous to the Agatha Christie detective story in popular literature, whose "solutions" to "mysteries" were the very essence of the deterministic view of nineteenth century mechanistic thought applied both to human actions and society.

In the age of Ruppelt then, "reality" was perceived as a series of planned development schedules within a totally mechanical *schema*. Time itself was the linear management of prototypal systems both in weaponry and consumerism, and already the two were beginning to overlap, becoming indistinguishable from one another. There was absolutely nothing that could not be measured and controlled and exploited to some industrial, scientific, technical, or consumer end. In this sense this was the very last phase of late Victorianism which some historians call the "modern" age. This age has been defined by some as the last era in which a thing displayed how it worked, how it came about, and what its precise function was. "Precise" is of course a much abused word in our own fuzzy post-industrial media-oriented world.

But compared to the nineteenth century, there was now emerging a fundamental difference. In the "modern" age of Ruppelt, belief was defined and structured not by costume, ceremony, religion or differences of social class, but by corporate scientism. As such, all human make-up and its manifest relations could theoretically be demystified; conflicts of any and every kind, whether in love, hatred, failure or sorrow could all be reduced to hard material analysis of connections between self and society. Ideally, "reality" defined as super-mechanism could not fail, or if it did, then it was through bad design or the special case of criminality or some other kind of corruption. This was all waste stuff, boundary layer conditions that did not alter the general formula that produced material success in everything and anything, and made the rest of the world feel as if they lived in a ditch and ate mud compared with chrome-bumper America. Techno-industrial enthusiasms replaced completely most religious enthusiasms. For the first time in history, you could have your inspirations and almost eat them.

As William H. Whyte pointed out in his 1956 book *The Organization Man*, this situation was a boon for the academic world. Shelves did indeed groan from weight of books discussing which output followed which input; there was not a set of causal relations that did not develop a veritable theology of equations. The most terrifying of these came from the Left, whose social-scientific rationalism in terms of behaviourist psychology and applied psychiatry resulted in the fascist horrors described in Ken Kesey's novel, *One Flew Over the Cuckoo's Nest*.

That technology and consumerism and indeed science itself were the re-fashioned tragic masks of timeless god-games was a debate not guaranteed exactly to reach intellectual primetime, and any entity that did not reach that gorgeous, pouting level was just beginning to be regarded as not quite "real."

But in the meantime, all was well for the prevailing Lords of Creation, the jet pilots, a few of whom would eventually reach the moon. Chuck Yeager describes the atmosphere in the Air Force at the time Ruppelt worked with ATIC:

> Being at Edwards in the 1950s, I was part of the greatest era in research flying in the history of aviation. In less than five years, a whole new air force was dumped in our laps for flight-testing. From first to last light, seven days a week, the desert sky over the Mojave thundered from new and powerful afterburners, an extra kick in the butt that shot us into the sky with a blast of flame and smoke. Man, we were at the centre of the world, the only place on earth to be if

you loved to fly. The old air force was being scrapped, and a new air force was being born right on our doorsteps.[13]

It was same feeling for Ruppelt, as for most Air Force men. He had a very happy marriage, a bouncing baby daughter, he worked regular hours, and he was happy to work under the user-friendly Rosengarten. Perhaps we can say that all was well with him until one day he heard the words "flying saucer" being used by some officers a few desks away from his own.

After that, as usual with the UFO effect, Ruppelt's world was never, ever the same again.

Enter the UFO

RUPPELT HAD NOT BEEN at ATIC very long when he first heard the words "flying saucer" used officially. He had heard a lot of talk about strange things in the sky, and indeed whilst serving as a bomber crewman, he had seen some strange things himself. Though at this time the books of George Adamski, such as *Flying Saucers Have Landed,* had not arrived, Ruppelt had almost certainly read the books of Frank Scully, such as *Behind the Flying Saucers* and Donald Keyhoe's *The Flying Saucers are Real*, both published in 1950. Inevitably, like almost every other American, he had a potted history of the flying saucer in his head from magazines, and indeed broadcasts and articles, from people such as Frank Edwards, a nationally known syndicated columnist and broadcaster from 1950 to 1954.

Whilst working on the Mig-15 project, Ruppelt was surprised to find out quite by accident that ATIC was responsible for receiving and analyzing UFO reports. James Rogers, the officer concerned with such sightings sat "three desks down and one over" from Ruppelt, who often took what little time off he could to eavesdrop on interesting conversations about UFOs.

In his book, Ruppelt always used inverted commas when referring to "expert" Rogers and the men around him. He watched the to-and-fro around this "expert's" desk with more than half an eye, and learned that Rogers constituted whole and entire the body of the then almost exhausted and quite ineffective Project Grudge.

His appetite thoroughly whetted by some of the things he heard, Ruppelt almost "sprung an eardrum" listening. He noted also that he had to listen to a considerable amount of rather red necked laughter concerning this subject.

This reaction was a typical one within military circles. The UFO had appeared at the very beginning of the start of growing confidence in the power of technology throughout the Western world. But from 1947 onwards, the UFO made increasing unannounced stage-entrances, and it rained on many a parade of military and scientific confidence. At first, humanity reacted to reports of UFO sightings rather as a dog puts its head on one side when hearing high-pitched sounds. The utterly strange manifestation of the "flying saucer," as it was then called, appeared at a time when scientific confidence and success was reaching its peak in the Western world. These beliefs reinforced the thought that at last humanity had instruments that could conquer not only space but pain and suffering, could create wealth and prosperity through proper rational management of all and everything. In other words, Tragedy and all that meant as regards Tillyard's view of the Renaissance cosmos could possibly be finally avoided by being engineered around, if not "solved" completely. Science was hence the "systems solution" to the metaphysical questions posed by the theory of Tragedy, the study of which was to occupy less and less of a place within the new "technological" universities.

But though the UFO appeared to have some kind of technological character (it was probably not a plant or an animal), its behaviour could not be predicted, and its "performance" could only be partly measured. It was thus out of all evolving conception and control and, since it appeared at a time when American material confidence was getting into gear, its presence was anything but welcome.

THE LAUGHTER WAS unusually loud from Rogers' quarter one particular day and Ruppelt describes the reported incident that appeared to have caused this mirth. The previous night, a Mid-Continent Airlines DC-3 (an aircraft very little changed from the twin-engine transport of wartime fame known by the British as the Dakota) took off from Sioux City Iowa *en route* for Omaha. Within minutes, after seeing strange bluish-white lights, the crew found themselves almost on a dead-ahead collision course with an object they described as looking like a wingless "fuselage of a B-29." The object flashed by their right wing, and a very short while later it appeared again, this time flying in steady formation with them.

A full Colonel from military intelligence happened to be on board the plane. He had seen the object, and he had made a report that arrived quickly at ATIC. Ruppelt described the official reaction to this report as a "great big, deep belly laugh." This puzzled him, because he had heard that the USAF was "seriously investigating all UFO reports."

Though he had only been at ATIC for a few weeks, Ruppelt was obviously a good observer and interpreter of men and events. It was at this point that he found himself at the entrance to the UFO rabbit-hole. After eavesdropping for a further "whole day" (how innocent the world was then!), he discovered that the "investigation" of the "UFO expert" consisted of a wire to Flight Service enquiring whether the sighting was of our old friend, a B-36 bomber, of all things.

This was Ruppelt's first shock at ATIC. Something about this school dorm giggling and low mental level offended both his maturity and his active intellect. His comment was:

> I certainly didn't class myself as an intelligence expert, but it didn't take an expert to see that a B-36, even one piloted by an experienced idiot, could not do what the UFO had done — buzz a DC-3 that was in an airport traffic pattern.[14]

Since the wingspan of a B-36 was over 500 feet (!) and the crew said the object did not have any wings at all, then this must have been Ruppelt's first encounter with something he had probably not experienced or even thought about before — cultural double-think. He was later to find that such double think was the one single thread that connected all his UFO investigations, and certainly it was a phenomenon quite as strange as the UFO itself, and just as disturbing. This effect still manifests itself over half a century later to the same degree. So much so, indeed, that it is now regarded as part of the UFO syndrome itself. It appears that rejection and denial of anomalistic events is a natural thing, generated by the event itself, and not through people being sick, maladjusted, mentally ill, or particularly unintelligent; many just shut off whole planes and vectors of experience that they cannot manage or do not want to know about for some reason. Thus the UFO is ghettoized as a most disturbing manifestation. This is an effect well analyzed by Charles Fort,[15] who lists many sightings of UFOs over the centuries. Scepticism in Fortean terms is a vital mental function, not so much to sort out truth from fiction, but to limit experience in order to make it manageable.

The denial of something that is right in front of the eyes is a very common kitchen phenomenon. The officer concerned in putting forward the B-36 theory was not so much incompetent - more likely, he blanked out an event that in his terms could not possibly occur and was therefore an utterly ridiculous thing not worthy of any kind of serious consideration. In the sense that for a moment he has stopped thinking in any meaningful sense, he is only half-alive. Rather an uncomplimentary view of the human condition yes, but human beings have had to face far worse truths about themselves than the revelation that most of us in our image-drenched Entertainment State are already almost dead, as far as thought independent of media images is concerned.

Ruppelt was puzzled. A few weeks later, he asked an ATIC veteran about the Sioux City Incident, and got the following reply, which he says "was typical of official policy at that time":

> One of these days one of these pilots will kill themselves, the crazy people on the ground will be locked up, and there won't be any more flying saucer reports.[16]

Yet he found that such attitudes were not unanimous. It was this difference in attitudes that deepened his interest in the subject, though professionally at this time he was not concerned with UFOs at all:

> The one thing that stood out to me, being unindoctrinated in the ways of UFO lore, was the schizophrenic approach so many people at ATIC took. On the surface they sided with the belly-laughers on any saucer issue, but if you were alone with them and started to ridicule the subject, they defended it, or at least took an active interest. I learned this one day after I had been at ATIC about a month.[17]

He asked a friend why there was such obvious forced negativity around. Since at this time Pearl Harbor was still very much ingrained in the American military character, it seemed odd and even dangerous to Ruppelt that vital information about a possible airborne threat (whatever that threat might be, alien or otherwise) was being ignored in such a manner. His friend replied, somewhat bitterly, "The powers-that-be are anti-flying saucer, and to stay in favour it behoves one to follow suit." Ruppelt adds: "As of February of 1951 this was the UFO project."

UFO A-Team

THE CONSTANT BARRACK-ROOM laughter from the Rogers UFO "research" group changed into almost hysterical fear one day when it became known that journalist Bob Ginna was investigating UFO sightings for an article in *Life* magazine. As far as Rogers was concerned, Ginna had started off a worrying chain of enquiry by going to the Office of Public Information in the Pentagon and enquiring about the current status of Project Grudge. *Life* magazine being the most influential journal in the nation at this time, Rogers was not happy at all when OPI sent a wire to ATIC asking about the current status of Project Grudge. Other reporters had enquired, but they did not get further than the top brass and learned nothing. Ruppelt, his tongue very much in cheek, sums up the ATIC response:

> Everything is under control; each new report is being thoroughly analyzed by our experts; our vast files of reports are in tip-top shape; and in general things are hunky-dunky. All UFO reports are hoaxes, hallucinations, and the misidentification of known objects.[18]

But the astute Ginna countered by getting the Pentagon to let him visit the Grudge Project at Dayton. As he told Ruppelt much later, his suspicions were correct. Rogers was completely incompetent. He had no knowledge and less intelligence, and the files were in absolute chaos. When Ginna arrived, the scene at ATIC was pure Laurel and Hardy as described by Ruppelt:

> Ginna had a long list of questions about reports that had been made over the past four years and every time he asked a question, the "expert" would go tearing out of the room to try to find the file that had the answer. I remember that day people spent a lot of time ripping open bundles of files and pawing through them like a bunch of gophers. Many times, "I'm sorry that's classified," got ATIC out of a tight spot.

Ginna left not at all impressed, with Rogers under a fatal cloud.

After that, things improved. Some two months later, Project Grudge was taken over by an extremely competent enlisted officer, Lieutenant W. Cummings of ATIC, and in September 1951, after nearly nine months at ATIC, Ruppelt was asked to give some part-time help to Cummings who, like Rogers before him, was running Project Grudge quite single-handed. The demands of the Korean War had drained ATIC of manpower, and Cummings was badly in need of help, particularly from someone like Ruppelt, who by this time had a reputation as one of the best systems-organizers at ATIC.

Thus was a small but effective UFO A-Team formed within ATIC. But this intrepid pair had to keep their heads down as far as those above the user-friendly Rosengarten were concerned, such as Colonel Watkins.

Ruppelt worked almost by the side of Cummings, and so he began to get "a UFO indoctrination via bull sessions." In those days, the idea of active field investigation of UFO sightings by Air Force officers was almost unheard of. Cummings' main task on the UFO project was somewhat passive. His desk job task was to try and go through as many files as he could and try and sift the "good" reports (radar, pilot visuals) from the "bad," which meant of course reports of abductions, purple-robed aliens and visions from mountaintops.

We note that even at this early stage in the history of the UFO, a common psychosocial filter was being rigidly applied, as in most "scientific" investigations. It is an amazing feature of the Western mind that those people who have had a UFO experience of any kind are judged to be people least worthy of analyzing that experience. The courts of "proper" debate rule out any odd, highly individualized, comic, or ludicrous or absurd elements. Here we see the most tragi-comic emblem of mankind's philosophy: get rid of the nutcases and there will be revealed the shining truth. Only the better-educated bourgeoisie can and will measure "reality" and say, daylight discs yes, controlled craft possibly; but occupants no! At least not yet. Only the clever and the sensible and those of social merit are worthy of meeting the gods. And they must prepare very carefully.

Life on distant stars? Yes. Then in water in Mars? Almost certainly. Then in molecules in earth-meteorites? Perhaps. Contact? We don't know yet. Abductions? No.

Thus does the alien tiptoe towards us along scales of allowances and rehearsals until the liminal event hatches out come seedtime.

We can only hope that alien denials, evasions, and illusions have by that time not evolved into weapons more potent than their B-Feature ray guns.

Destruction of the Evidence

OCCASIONALLY CUMMINGS would toss a "good" report over to Ruppelt's desk. The incident at White Sands Proving Ground[19] in New Mexico on April 27, 1950 was an example, and illustrates the scaling down of an event such as to almost obliterate it in time. White Sands was where the first test firing of ex-German V2 rockets took place, and by 1950 it was a well-developed missile range of many square miles in area, fully equipped with cinetheodolite instrumentation, special cameras and good communications.

On this date, a missile had been fired, and as it fell back from the stratosphere to Earth, camera crews had recorded its flight. The crews were about to leave the area when one of them spotted an object "streaking across the sky." Ruppelt says that by April 1950 "every person at White Sands was UFO-conscious," and consequently, another member of the crew grabbed a telephone handset and alerted others of the team, telling them to take pictures. Unfortunately, only one of the cameras had film in it and before film could be loaded again, the UFO was gone. The film that was shot showed an indistinct blur, just sufficient to show that indeed a moving body was present before the lens, but little else could be obtained from the image.

A year later, Ruppelt got in touch with the Data Reduction Group at White Sands. As with Project Grudge under Rogers, the files were in chaos.[20] Ruppelt was however fortunate enough to contact a Major who talked to the laboratory staff, and made a report, which he gave to Ruppelt:

> The Major said that by putting a correction factor in the data gathered by the two cameras they were able to arrive at a rough estimate of speed, altitude, and size. The UFO was "higher than 40,000 feet, travelling over 2,000 miles per hour, and it was over 300 feet in diameter."[21]

As is the common way with many things Ufological, when Ruppelt enquired, the photographs of this White Sands sighting had been lost.

The loss of UFO evidence over the years is a major theme of the UFO story. Photographs, drawings, reports, camera and video film, whenever these things enter the UFO area, they appear to enter a permanently unstable region where reference, definition, and materiality become so doubtful that this body of "evidence" consists of the kind of Max Escher "impossible" objects discussed in the next chapter. Human beings too, disappear and/or do things quite against their nature in the field of influence of the UFO. Readers might like to read for instance Donald Keyhoe's account[22] of the strange resignation in 1965 from NICAP of Vice Admiral Hillenkoeter, USN, the UFO researcher who was an ex-head of the CIA, of all things.

The wilful destruction of UFO evidence is just one of the most profound and disturbing aspects of the phenomenon. For instance, Colonel Watson perversely destroyed wire recordings of the Pentagon conference organized by his chief, Major-General Cabell, an affair discussed later in this book. This conference (attended by Rosengarten and Cummings) was a full discussion of the Fort Monmouth UFO incident, and the recording of the proceedings represented an important UFO Intelligence archive.

When an Intelligence chief (of all people) wilfully destroys official evidence of this kind, something else is in operation other than prejudice, dislike, or plain ignorance, and we can rule out carelessness. Like a good chemist, under normal conditions no Intelligence man ever destroys anything upon pain of death. Intelligence, minus the James Bond bit, is about bureaucracy and office clerking, particularly in those days when there were no significant computers available. In making the rather risky assumption that no one above him in rank (or indeed otherwise) was ever going to ask for the recording either in part or in whole or in transcript version, Watson took an amazing gamble with his reputation. He acted not only against his own survival instincts (strongly developed in a fighter ace!) but also against sound Intelligence procedures, and probably indeed against Air Force Law. If he acted on a single, ill-thought, prejudiced impulse, he was risking possible reprimand, demotion, dismissal from the Air Force. In destroying Air Force property, he risked the criminal proceedings of a Court Martial. Moreover, Watson did this when, pending a transfer to Germany, he was no longer in charge at ATIC, having been replaced by Colonel Frank Dunn, and therefore he had no authority to touch anything at ATIC at all.

But perhaps he was following the example of his peers in this respect. For example, General Hoyt Vandenberg, Chief of Staff of the Air Force in 1948, destroyed the legendary "Estimate of the Situation." This was a UFO report made by the Project Sign Group in late July 1948. This Group came to the conclusion that the UFOs were interplanetary vehicles. Though the very existence of this "Estimate" has been denied many times by Air Force officials, Ruppelt himself says he saw a copy:

> It was rather a thick document with a black cover and it was printed on legal-sized paper. Stamped across the front were the words TOP SECRET.[23]

According to Ruppelt's testimony again, this was the type of material the "Estimate" contained, prior to its being incinerated a few months after receipt:

> It contained the Air Force's analysis of many of the incidents I have told you about plus many similar ones. All of them had come from scientists, pilots, and other equally credible observers, and each one was an unknown.

He continues:

> The general wouldn't buy interplanetary vehicles. The report
> lacked proof. A group from ATIC went to the Pentagon to bolster
> their position but had no luck; the Chief of Staff just couldn't be
> convinced. Some months later the report was completely declassified
> and relegated to the incinerator. A few copies, one of which I saw,
> were kept as reminders of the golden days of the UFOs.[24]

As in the Watson example above, we have to ask ourselves why, UFOs apart, such a mass of detailed evidence was destroyed in any case. Was not such a thing of general Intelligence interest in any case? Would it not have been prudent to leave it in the top secret files for possible future reference? Supposing the President or some other person in high office had wanted to hear the recording or see the "Estimate" after it had been destroyed? These destructive actions are again most unusual for any top executive in any business anywhere, almost all of whom take good care to cover their tracks and watch their backs very carefully. In destroying what they destroyed, both Watson and Vandenberg laid themselves open to grave charges.

Richard Dolan[25] gives several examples of human beings applying an almost implicit censorship rather than an explicit one. The UFO is air-brushed out of their reality scheme as an automatically conditioned response, erased rather like the faces of errant Soviet commissars in photographs of the Supreme Soviet and limitless Communist committees in the 1950s and 1960s.

He gives the examples of Admiral Hillenkoeter's amazing decision to quit the US organization NICAP (National Investigations Committee on Aerial Phenomena) in 1962,[26] and also examples of "straight" biographers of famous men who have left out the (often very public) association of these men with UFO organizations. In these cases, no finite security organization, no matter how vast, powerful, or meticulous, could penetrate to the very interstices of consciousness where such deep instructions dwell, activated, in this author's opinion, by the approach of a liminal event. Hillenkoeter's turn-about action was so peculiar it was psychologically equivalent to tearing up a whole identity, amounting to complete laceration of his public face. Here, (though Dolan mentions no such thing) to this present author, David Icke's lizards are not very far away, at least metaphorically.

The Secret of Invisibility

IN THIS SENSE, THESE STRANGE actions by clever, sane, practical men with their feet very much on the ground are like B-Feature metaphors in action. Traditionally, these films show many examples of evidence being lost, and show people in authority not being at all what they seem.

The B-story goes something like this. The main character, we'll call him John, goes to Davis, a man in high authority to tell him about aliens. John's impression of Davis is that he is "solid reality," a kind of moral bedrock by means of which all illusions can be measured and brought to nothing. Unlike John, the audience guesses rightly that this paste-up father figure of Science and Authority, like the great white bearded God in the sky, is as phoney as silicon tits, but just as an orphaned monkey in a zoo thinks a hot water bottle is its mother, John thinks his dad is "real." John is sure that his photographs, reports, and interviews and samples and documentation will be studied and returned. He leaves, confident that he has done the right thing. Shot to interior: Davis reveals he is a lizard form. End of scene: the photographs, witness-interviews and reports are shown being thrown into an incinerator.

Every second book on UFOs over a half century has some version of the end of this story, in which John returns to try and see Davis. But no one has heard of the man he met, his department, or the office John saw. John then receives mysterious telephone calls telling him to investigate no further. Months later John, having a cup of coffee on the sidewalk, sees Davis walk by. He runs after him, but the mysterious man disappears in a maze of alleys and doorways, and John sees neither Davis nor his material again.

Such a night-side of anomalistic experiences was in existence long before 1947 and Kenneth Arnold's first sighting of "flying saucers." Time and again the main themes of Orwell, Kafka, and Charles Fort are almost identical to UFO themes. The ideas of implicit control in the books of these writers often overshadow ideas of explicit control. The actual castle in Kafka's novel *The Castle* can be looked upon as one huge permanently grounded UFO, with Men in Black going in and out of it by the score. These creatures (rather like the agents in the *Matrix* films) carry the inevitable briefcases concerning "evidence" about partial "truths" about personality and identity, and especially claims for "reality." Kafka's Josef K. is told that his trial was opened long before he was born, and will continue indefinitely, even after his death.

Like Hillenkoeter, and the evidence-burners Vandenburg and Watson, Josef K. is a series of masks, any one of which may take control at any one time.

OF COURSE IF WE were to see Watson or Vandenberg destroying the evidence we would (most probably!) not see a lizard face. The lizard face, from the early B-Features to David Icke, is symbolic of that conditioning paradigm circuitry that makes us do things we are only partly conscious of, or do not want to do in the first place. The "alien instruction" is present as a piece of viral information activated under certain circumstances. This is the implicit conspiracy, as distinct from the explicit. We have no problem in admitting that our bodies are robotically programmed, but we have very great difficulty in admitting the same of our mental faculties. Just like Josef K. and Orwell's Winston Smith, we like to think we are free of all implicit agendas. It is unlikely that we are, since every single one of us is now watching round-the-clock TV whether we have a set or not.

As the works of Orwell and Kafka show us, there is no OFF switch.

As we shall see in this book, such strange actions and events are almost without count as regards the giving of evidence to Authority, quite outside the realm of the B-Feature. Sceptics and believers alike, when they come near the UFO field, behave in a strange way as if they have been switched on by a highly selective impulse, and they do things that they would never do under normal circumstances. This super-state of mind, as it were, does not last very long; it does not affect them deeply and permanently. In a second they open or close a door, as if their actions were determined by the very fast application of a very narrow bandwidth of a most singular programme, that has nothing to do with anything else but the opening and closing of that particular mental door.

As any secret agent will tell us, the secret of success in this profession is not to look like James Bond, but to look like absolutely nothing at all.

This is the secret of invisibility.

The negative reaction to certain aspects of the UFO phenomenon has always been an essay in the psychology of denial. In the anthropology of Western techno-shamanism, denial is not so much an attempt to demonstrate that a thing is true or untrue, but to render it invisible: that is, to de-propagandize its image in media time. From the very beginning, that is from Kenneth Arnold's UFO sighting on June 24, 1947, denials of the existence of UFOs have always had a special quality. Such denials do not appear to come from that natural human rejection response essential for filtering out palpable nonsense. No, more like there is the lightning slam of some mental door, an action so fast that the normal processes of consciousness hardly detect it. There appears to be no processing between perception and rejection, no separating out, as with other qualities, of the good, the bad or the indifferent parts. Then and now, most UFO sceptical denials are almost completely implicit, pre-conditioned, almost as if they were some quite automatic function of a bio-electric switch, shutting off certain planes of information within the brain.

As with many believers, in few sceptics do we find considered intellectual rejection. Rather do we find quite genuine anger and resentment and bitterness, as if the phenomenon not only offends them intellectually, but also offends some deep, very private thing which they hold dear. Give a man like Colonel Watson an airplane, and he would see immediately the good, bad and indifferent parts of this machine; give him the very best of UFO sightings and he would not see any such distinct qualitative shading. He would not separate it out (as would be expected) in the same manner.

We humans are highly selective creatures; no purple robes on mountaintops please, we're scientists. Of course, should any self-respecting alien know of this filter, the first thing he or she (or it or other) would provide for themselves would be the very best purple robes and mountain tops they could lay their scaly hands upon. The key to all invisibility lies here: find the mental cut-off points and you are free to do as you please.[27]

Fifty years later, many sceptics on this level are switched off like a light bulb in similar fashion. For all the world it is as if some paradigm-operated bioelectric relay contact has received a fast set of instructions, B-Feature robot style. We shall meet many more examples of this strange, automated mental switching as we proceed in this book. The UFO phenomenon is about people and societies as much as it is about whatever it is in itself.

The New Ufology

IN ANALYSING THE PECULIAR changes in personality discussed previously, there is a need to construct a New Ufology which gets away from the passive listing of countless case histories from the past. Ufological studies should be integrated with the latest developments in psychology and mathematics, along with up-to-date Postmodern views on Artificial Intelligence and Image Processing.

The anomalistic UFO resembles above all things, the drawing of a concept by Roger Penrose[28] (**figure 1**). Penrose (working with his father) created his "impossible" triangle under the influence of M.C. Escher.[29] Escher put objects into estranged perspectives from which, like Penrose, he removed certain strands of spatial information.

The effect is one of disorientation, rather like a feeling of an object being very near and very far away at the same time. Putting the hands to the eyes, and looking through slits in the fingers at the drawing room table can induce this effect, and the surface of the table appears to be miles away, but seems to exist in many dimensions at once. These drawings fulfil all the classical Fortean conditions for an information-based model of artificial intelligence.

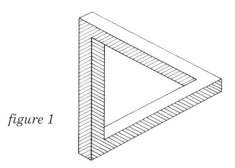

figure 1

The figure is composed of square beams which rest upon each other at right-angles. If we follow the various parts of this construction one by one, we are unable to discover any mistakes in it. Yet it is an impossible whole because changes occur suddenly in the interpretation of distances between our eye and the object. In that this triangle lies, therefore, between fact and fiction, it is the kind of liminal object discussed in this book.

The drawing by Escher illustrated below (**figure 2**) is a very good emblem for how we process anomalies such as the UFO. Many cases of UFO observation and experience combine a kind of brief psychological distortion and height-fear, as if the observer is about to fall through the floor of the world, as it were.

We steady ourselves as regards the UFO experience, therefore, as we steady ourselves from tripping up by reaching for the nearest solid object. We hardly intellectualize such a reach for safety; some reaction takes over with an alacrity that is hardly consciously processed.

A Chain of Being

The energy for this typical and nervously fearful reaction is supplied by the clash of similar mental confusions to those aroused by Escher-Penrose figures and drawings. First, observers see a common object, but then realize quickly that the object, though familiar, is not quite of this world. We try to make the appropriate adjustments but we cannot do so. We are left in a state of momentary stress, a kind of vertigo as what we see combines several viewpoints in one experience (or print), and the spectator has the sensation of viewing the scene simultaneously from above, below, and from different spatial foci and mental resolution.

figure 2

But the Western mind has some difficulty in conceiving of what Postmodernists call a liminal object: that is, something hovering between past and future, real and unreal, fact and fiction. Yet we hallucinate, rehearse, act-out purely mental stage-sets, "factual" frameworks and "hard" distinctions as a form of psychological management to help navigate approximately through all the approximations that make up the world. Like the steam engine, the germ and the cell, the atom and the molecule were indeed once such liminal things, being intermediate states half-in and half-out of directly received experience, before being brought centre-stage in cultural primetime and equated to some theoretical "real."

Such liminal forms as the UFO abound throughout history. It would have been possible to find the steam engine in 1760, but it was a liminal form strung between fact and fiction; it was a set of almost-ideas spread through the time like salmon paste on rye. It "existed" in the form of correspondence, conversations, drawings and sketches, intuitions and dreams, plus the start of a few strange bangs (and not a few explosions as the strength of early boiler seams were tested) down dark, greasy alleyways where respectable people did not go. We can deconstruct the birth of the germ, the steam engine, or Arkwright's Spinning Jenny as a film run rapidly forwards. First, our liminal object spreads thinly through the universe. Each starts as a kind of embryo creature made of rumour, information dumps, images, and suggestions, propaganda and folklore. The virtual stage is the larval stage. Out of this rich nutrient of rehearsals, approximations, the intermediate stage or half-form emerges like the atom of Rutherford, William Hedley's Puffing Billy of 1812, the germ-forms of Joseph Lister and Louis Pasteur, or unfortunately the meme-forms of the dialectics of Karl Marx and Adolf Hitler.

A UFO EXPERIENCE THEN, being liminal, is half-in, half-out of the Cartesian frame, making it a most peculiar thing that exists in the intermediate area between fact and fiction.

The important thing about the Escher-Penrose object and the UFO is that neither can be fully "measured" in the proper sense. Our difficulties with such intermediate states of belief and matter vary according to the state and strength and complexity of our mental resources. Socially, all such anomalies in the Fortean sense are a problem, and scientifically they are meaningless and absurd. If we dismiss the UFO as a fiction, then there are numberless group-observations, radar traces, and a certain amount of physical evidence; if we claim UFOs as facts, then we cannot account for their behaviour, just as we cannot account for lack of a detectible food swathe for Bigfoot or the Yeti, creatures that would require massive daily intakes of food. The film *The Matrix* and the book *Techgnosis* by Erik Davis are an indication of this emerging view of liminality.

Further, the "physical evidence" for both UFO and Bigfoot more often than not bleeds away as if indeed UFO and Bigfoot belong to our world only as partial and somewhat indeterminate constructions. Films blur, samples get lost, and what appear to be automatically generated warnings (Black helicopters, Men in Black) appear. A purely linear mechanistic view will see all such manifestations as "noise in the system," "explained" as the result of paranoia, hallucinations, and misinterpretations. But if we take the Postmodern view that every single aspect of consciousness and experience is built of different forms of networked information, then the Escher-Penrose figure becomes a possible model for a new kind of information state that might give us a clue to the most peculiar nature of the UFO experience. It offers also a chance for Ufology to get out of the rut of that static archive mind-set which produces lists of case histories and little else instead of original critical analysis.

This author (who has had a most profound UFO experience in the past) is now inclined to accept the inter-dimensional hypothesis rather than the extra-terrestrial one. When both mind and intelligence are viewed as operational media entities, the "worm hole" and "stargate" ideas of physicists such as Jack Sarfatti and Eric Davis appear as direct analogies to the Escher-Penrose information state.

Photographs and physical items (and on occasion cattle and people) all disappear within the UFO experience framework, almost as if they were built of suggestions, the software of acts and temporary performances rather than of molecules and atoms. Like Escher-Penrose objects, such "evidence" appears only partly to belong to this world.

I propose an Escher-Penrose state as a model for a new theory of information processing regarding the UFO. In the sense that we are about to examine things that may belong to this world only in part, we are therefore about to take a look at a possible Escher-Penrose state.

Fighting the Syndicate

NEITHER HIS DEGREE in aeronautical engineering nor the War had prepared Ruppelt for meeting explanations that were more fantastic than the thing they were trying to explain, and it is a tribute to him that he persevered with his view under often difficult circumstances. By 1951, most people knew that UFOs were not from the Soviet Union; they knew they were not a US aircraft prototype, nor a prototype of any other nation.

Throughout the summer of 1951, both Ruppelt and Lieutenant Cummings "fought the syndicate," trying to make the UFO respectable within ATIC:

> All the time I was continuing to get my indoctrination. Then one day with the speed of a shotgun wedding, the long-overdue respectability arrived. The date was September 12, 1951, and the exact time was 3:04 PM.[30]

At this exact date and time an Operation Immediate order came through by Teletype to Wright Patterson, and was delivered by special messenger to ATIC. The report was from the Army Signal Corps radar centre at Fort Monmouth, New Jersey. It was as Ruppelt says, "red hot," and it told the following story.

At 11:18 am on Monday September 10, 1951 an astonishing event had occurred. At Fort Monmouth Radar School, on the coastline of New Jersey, a young student Army Signal Corps radar operator, PFC Clark, was giving a radar demonstration to a group of high-ranking Air Force officers. His set was a modified AN/MPG-1 capable of operating in the lower Gigahertz band, which was high for those days. Most of such equipment at this time came from war reserve stocks and, though much-modified, it was still pretty crude compared to such equipment in our own day. The circuitry was full of soldered-on post-war modifications, more afterthoughts from technicians anxious to get back to civilian life than to involve themselves in vast post-war programmes of new design and development.

That said, the radars of the early 1950s contained basic components, some of which have not changed much in a half century. The basic high-frequency amplifier of those days was one of several US versions of the British cavity magnetron, whose unique internal resonator was one of the great secrets of WWII, given to America by the British in exchange for such things as the proximity fuse. Going back to ATIC during Ruppelt's time, we would recognise the box-like wave-guides, and an array of various kinds and sizes of aerials, including fixed horns and steerable parabolic dishes. The equipment, capable of operating at within the 2–10 cm region at a few hundred watts to as high as 40,000 feet, would be warm to the touch, and the rising heat from its glowing vacuum tubes would give the units the pyramid smell of a different age. We would see a few manually operated filter circuits for anomalous returns such as weather, sea conditions, and temperature inversions, but these were analogue circuits, mere selective pulse cut-outs, not synthesized from a memory.

The transistor had only just emerged from the laboratories at this time, and almost all US Armed Forces equipment used relatively slow-return vacuum-tube technology all of which was analogue, but nevertheless, the radar in this case was quite capable of picking up with reasonable definition the subsonic military jets of this time. None of the equipment (including of course the screen) was digitized, and therefore what an operator saw in those days was very much what he (or she) was getting. Consequently, an operator had to become extremely skilled both in recognition and interpretation of what the raw screen returns showed, since there was very little equipment to help them do so automatically.

In this case, the operator happened to be demonstrating automatic tracking. This was new in those days, and was the radar equivalent to the semi-automatic pilot in an aircraft. This hands-off operating allowed the operator to concentrate more on interpreting the screen situation, and was far less exhausting than the constant manual manipulation of the war years. It was also the beginning of that technology which allowed radar to handle and control more than one target on a single screen, and therefore what was being shown was new technology for the time.

The operator demonstrated manual tracking at first, showing the traces of local air traffic. He then informed his audience that he was going to switch to automatic tracking to let them see how this worked.

Before he could do so however, before the eyes of the operator and his attentive (and very knowledgeable) audience, a well-defined blip appeared on the screen about 12,000 yards southeast of the station, flying low towards the north, traversing the coastline at an estimated speed of 700 mph. This meant that the object was moving faster than any known jet aircraft of the time.

PFC Clark switched immediately to automatic tracking, but the object was too fast for the tracking. It must be borne in mind here that "tracking" meant of course the movement of heavy external aerial assemblies by means of servo-electric hydraulics. These rigs could move fast enough for subsonic speeds but, grounded in WWII technology, they were not designed to follow anything near or above Mach 1. Another problem was the slow speed of vacuum-tube (valve) circuitry compared with the coming transistor circuitry.

The target was visible for a full three minutes before it disappeared from the scope in a northerly direction, and during that time it could not be automatically tracked. This meant that it had no difficulty in maintaining near Mach 1 performance in an area criss-crossed by civilian air routes. Unfortunately, in these pre-video days there was no ready and useful means of recording radar returns. Film equipment was available on occasion on test ranges, but it was expensive, cumbersome, temperamental, and required the full-time specialized care demanded by a small bad-tempered child. As such, there are very few visual records of radar returns of occasions such as this.

Finally, the target went off the scope near the Sandy Hook coastal peninsula not far south of New York City.

All parties were deeply embarrassed by what they had seen. The high-ranking officers were as impressed as the controller, and prepared to go back to their bases to write reports that would ask many troublesome questions.

But before they had time to get back to their separate headquarters, another dramatic incident occurred in the skies over New Jersey, exactly twenty five minutes after this morning sighting.

First-Lieutenant Wilbert S. Rogers of the 148th Interceptor Squadron took off in a T33 jet trainer from Dover Air Force Base, Delaware, and headed towards Mitchel Air Force Base, New York. His passenger in the rear seat was Major Edward Ballard Jr. Just south of Sandy Hook, at 11:35 the two men both observed a dull silver disc below them. The weather was perfectly clear, and the T33 was at 20,000 feet above Point Pleasant, New Jersey. Rogers was an experienced WWII fighter pilot, and his estimate was that the thirty–forty foot disk was passing on an opposing parallel course 12,000 feet far below them. Rogers had been on an approach heading into Mitchel AFB, with Ballard on the radio. Ballard now saw the disc, and the two men's reactions were heard over an open r/t microphone.

The disk now descended, southward bound from the coastline peninsula of Sandy Hook, and Rogers dived in hot pursuit, making a 360° turn as he did so. As he descended the disc, obviously now not a balloon, promptly stopped its own descent, stood still (!), made a 120° turn, and vanished out to sea. It covered thirty five miles during the two-minute duration of the sighting, making the disc speed an estimated 1,180 mph![31]

At 3.15 on this same day, the radar group at Fort Monmouth got a "frantic" call from HQ ordering them to try and pick up a target high to the north in the area where the last object vanished. They picked it up and reported that it was travelling slowly at 93,000 feet, that is eighteen miles above the Earth!

Ground observers saw it as a silver speck.

THE NEXT MORNING, as a brief summary of the T33 sighting made its way to ATIC, two radar sets picked up simultaneously yet another target that could not be tracked automatically. This performer would climb, level off, climb again, and go into a dive. That afternoon, radar tracked another unidentified slow moving object for several minutes.

On the following day, September 12, Ruppelt describes the reception of the message from Fort Monmouth:

> On this date and time a teletype machine at Wright-Patterson AFB began to chatter out a message. Thirty-six inches of paper rolled out of the machine before the operator ripped off the copy, stamped it Operational Immediate, and gave it to a special messenger to deliver

to ATIC. Lieutenant Cummings got the message. The report was from the Army Signal Corps radar centre at Fort Monmouth, New Jersey, and it was red-hot.[32]

Both date and time here are correct, but Lieutenant Cummings very definitely did not get the message. But then Ruppelt goes on to contract three incidents into the time frame of a single day:

Before Jerry [Cummings] could digest the thirty-six inches of facts, ATIC'S new chief, Colonel Frank Dunn, got a phone call. It came from the office of the Director of Intelligence of the Air Force, Major General (now Lieutenant General) Cabell. General Cabell wanted somebody from ATIC to get to New Jersey — fast — and find out what was going on. As soon as the reports had been thoroughly investigated, the general said that he wanted a complete personal report. Nothing expedites like a telephone call from a general officer, so in a matter of hours Lieutenant Cummings and Lieutenant-Colonel Rosengarten were on an airliner, New Jersey-bound.[33]

This time scheme is nonsense, but it was probably given at the time of writing in 1956 in order not to show the stupendous, oaf-like stupidity and inefficiency of parts of the ATIC Intelligence operation at the time of the Cold War. It was done also to conceal the conflicts between personalities within ATIC.

Fifty years later, researchers Hall and Connors have shown the story to be very different. There was a considerable time lapse between the Fort Monmouth incidents and the arrival of any significant Intelligence on Cabell's desk. For example, Dover AFB had officially reported the Fort Monmouth sightings to ATIC on the 11th and 12th, and the EADC (Eastern Air Defence Command) at Newburg had reported them on the 21st. But both accounts had been almost contemptuously received by Bruno W. Feiling of ATIC, who was apparently still following scrupulously the anti-UFO policy of his (previous) chief, Colonel Watson. Despite the Fort Monmouth report having an "Operational Immediate" category, Feiling delayed it by several days before delaying it still further by sending it to the incompetent Rogers (head of the original Project Grudge whom Cummings had replaced). Rogers, yet another camp follower of Colonel Watson, was convinced that "the whole outfit were a bunch of young impressionable kids, and the T33 crew had seen a [cockpit Perspex] reflection."[34]

The lack of integrated tactical definition within ATIC circles in these days is illustrated by the choice of Rogers as a suitable man to send such a report to. But since the report involved radar, it was sent to Rogers because he was the ATIC radar expert.

Such are the ways of bureaucracy. This was typical departmental thinking, pure category-administrative, with no broad based overview. The possible reason for this delaying action was that Feiling was probably playing for time, not wanting to show demonstrably to General Cabell that the run-down Grudge was being slowly strangled by Watson's anti-UFO party, and just about everybody else.

No wonder Ruppelt carefully concealed this mess. Knowing the opposing parties within ATIC over the issue of UFOs, they would have been of prime interest to Russian Intelligence who might well have exploited them.

The person proper to whom this report should have been sent was Rosengarten. He in turn would have given the report to Lieutenant Jerry Cummings, who did complain to both Dyarmond and Rosengarten that the Fort Monmouth report should have been given to him, so that Rosengarten did just that, taking the report from Feiling and giving it to Cummings.

The waste of time involved in this troubled and confusing bureaucratic transfer occupied the better part of a week, which leads us up to some time around September 20. Given that an analysis of the report, and the writing of a report on the original report, would take another six to seven days by Cummings, who had not a single full-time assistant, this leads us to the morning of Friday, September 28.

Two things happened on this day. ATIC received a blistering telephone call from Cabell himself calling for immediate action, since he was now something like two weeks out of touch with the Fort Monmouth incident! In the afternoon, ATIC received a long Teletype from AFOIN (Air Force Office of Intelligence) in similar vein at 4 pm which, according to Ruppelt, was ATIC's official "closing time." It shows what kind of innocent days these were when the USAF's Intelligence branch shut up shop at what the Brits call teatime!

Two men at the top level of ATIC then decided that something must be done immediately, or their very military careers could possibly be threatened. These men were Colonel S.H. Kirkland and Colonel Watson's good friend from wartime days, Moose Deyarmond. They decided that, due to pressure from the Pentagon, Cummings and Rosengarten should be dispatched immediately to Fort Monmouth and work without sleep if necessary in order to get a report to General Cabell in the Pentagon by Monday morning, October 1.

At 11:30 pm (EST) on Friday, September 28, Cummings and Rosengarten boarded a TWA commercial airliner and flew direct to

New York. Travelling to New Jersey the next morning, they interrogated Signal Corps personnel concerned in the sightings, working almost round the clock.

Next, 1st Lieutenant Rogers (no relation to the ATIC Rogers) and Major Edward Ballard flew to Mitchel AFB on Sunday 30th, and Rosengarten and Cummings travelled on from Fort Monmouth to interrogate them. Both pilot and passenger were convinced they had seen something intelligently controlled, and were dismissive of any suggestion that they had seen a balloon. Cummings himself visited the Air Defence Command radar site at Sandy Hook. He got a very cold B-Feature reception, and had to pull strings to get into the place. Hall and Connors quote from Ruppelt's unpublished manuscript:

> When he did [get in] he found out that things were all fouled up. The radar logs showed unidentified targets but the officer said that they were SAC [Strategic Air Command] on a classified training mission. The log didn't show this however. Jerry [Cummings] didn't think that he [the officer concerned] established that the radar had no other target other than the T33 at the time of the sighting.[35]

In view of this state of affairs, Cabell's bad mood before the meeting on October 1 was understandable. Obviously, there had been a catastrophe in prime Intelligence handling, along with a press leak. It was obvious that administration and command and control of the homeland air defence were in a dreadful mess, as illustrated by the following.

On September 11, a brief summary of the T33 sighting was sent to ATIC from the 148th interceptor group. The next day the pilot, 1st Lieutenant Rogers, himself sent a more detailed summary to ATIC, and in turn, Fort Monmouth Radar School sent in their reports of the anomalous radar returns. Additionally, both 1st Lieutenant Rogers and Major Ballard were debriefed on September 17 at Stewart AFB Newburg, New York by staff of the Eastern Air Defence Headquarters. On the 21st, this account was sent together with a summary of all the other sightings to ATIC as well as to the Air Defence Command HQ in Colorado Springs. All these reports were caught up in administrative delay and semi-deliberate parcel-passing by the anti-UFO staff, in particular Colonel Brunow and Feiling. The latter by-passed Grudge channels altogether and gave the reports to James Rogers, the not-too-bright anti-UFO radar "expert" met previously in this book, who was not well-disposed towards Ruppelt and Cummings. The result was that once again there was general chaos as regards the UFO, and it appears that no one knew what on earth they were doing, and cared even less.

Through similar bungling and inefficiency, there also occurred a press leak, which did not improve Cabell's temper. This leak came from Mitchel AFB when Major Barron allowed a Long Island journalist, Dick Aurelio, to interview Rogers, the pilot of the T33. Aurelio of course spread the news as far and as fast as he could about the sightings.

Thus the first Cabell knew of the sightings was when he read national headlines in the *Washington Daily News* and *The New York Times*. There had been some press cover of the Monmouth sightings as early as the 12th of this month, but Cabell did not appear to learn any of this until as late as the 27th or 28th.

Thus the reports had to pass through many filters of prejudice and delay before they reached Cabell. This was nothing like the zero response time required by a jet-age Intelligence agency whose speed of mental processing and action must by definition be as fast as is humanly possible.

The speed of any kind of processing and action here was at the pre-tank speed of 1914. The shambles during the UFO sightings over Washington some months later were to prove this yet again.

Cabell of course, as Chief of Air Force Intelligence, must have realized that he could get himself into serious trouble if things went on like this. He was, after all, no less than the major supplier of the body of technical Intelligence to the entire United States Air Force at a time of war in Korea. If it was felt by his superiors that he was falling down on any aspect of the job, no matter what that job was, his head could be put on the block very quickly indeed. Already, after the headlines, the Eastern Air Defence Command itself was screaming at him. They had not received a final report on the Monmouth sightings even though the pilots involved were part of this Command. Apparently unaware that Project Grudge was hardly operating at all as an organization, the EADC thought Grudge would get into action as a full and powerful team straight away.

In all fairness to those who believe that alien bodies and/or craft were recovered at Roswell in 1947, it must be said that given the creaking organization revealed here, it certainly doesn't look as if these inefficient and quarrelling administrative amateurs handled such a thing! If the Roswell events occurred (and this author thinks that indeed they did, in some form or other) then the entire alien/craft recovery operation must have been by quite a different (possibly hybrid) outfit altogether.

Library shelves have been filled with speculations on this issue.

The idea that humanity might interact with some other intelligent animal agency, operating in a shadow-like dimension alongside human affairs, is just about the most disturbing idea of our time.

Of course this "living alongside" idea might be more psychologically disturbing to us than a full-scale, H.G. Wells type alien invasion, or the realization that the culture above us is as varied as the culture below us.

Cabell had yet other problems. For some time he had been under pressure from industrialists and scientists urging greater efforts as regards UFO investigation by the Air Force. These civilians were wholly free to speak their mind and act, as distinct from servicemen within a military organization.

At this time Republic Aviation had two men at the top who were very interested in UFOs. These men were Robert Johnson and a Mr. Brewster of Republic Aircraft Corporation. The latter was almost certainly a scion of the Brewster family, who gave their name to another famous American aircraft company (defunct after 1945) that manufactured the Brewster Buffalo fighter, a machine of somewhat mixed reputation. Air Force files show that these men knew of the Fort Monmouth case, and indeed had asked the Eastern Air Defence Command for permission to speak to Rogers and Ballard long before Cabell had been briefed on the incidents. Thus as distinct from the bureaucratic, slow minded military, it can be seen that the civilian sector was moving in quickly, complete with studies, questions and information. These men were not disinterested military time-servers such as Rogers, but the kind of scientist-engineer investigators proper that Cabell finally saw that he needed in ATIC. Johnson and Brewster were very intelligent, extremely well educated and highly qualified men. They had developed intellects, and were open-minded. Compared to high powered investigators of this calibre, the military were absolutely hopeless boy scouts. These were the kind of men that Ruppelt, to his eternal credit, recruited as advisors when he became head of Blue Book later in 1951.

Round about October 20, Johnson and Brewster were given permission by Eastern Air Defence Command to interview Rogers and Ballard. This shows how a high level civilian technological sector had been gathering UFO information on its own initiative. That this cell was in existence at all meant, surely, that other such cells were working on the same problem. Thus we have a rare glimpse of how the threads of the military industrial complex worked alongside the civilian dimension at this time. The Air Force had the technological muscle, but its brain and intellectual resources were severely restricted, it being essentially a strategic fighting force, and not an out-of-the-box think-tank like the Rand Corporation or the Beacon Hill Group (discussed later). As with any military organization, it was not particularly fond of enterprise and imagination as compared with civilian organizations, and they themselves restricted such things enough! However, the Rogers/Ballard interview is a good early example of how closely-linked but semi-dependent and separate threads were beginning to merge within a common techno-industrial base in the immediate post-War world.

Unbelievably, this interview was some ten days before Cabell was briefed. The civilians were acting fast; they were in the right place at the right time, asking the right questions. It is sad to think that Blue Book would never ever have been able to operate like this all by itself, even if it had been given the very best of support and conditions.

Hall and Connors[36] show how extensive was this private initiative:

> During their interview, Brewster showed the crew "sketches," possibly of experimental aircraft. Yet both pilots told Brewster and Johnson that they had seen no indications of exhaust or propulsion units on the UFO. Records even show Brewster speculative of electrical propulsion of some kind. Brewster explained that he had names of other witnesses — who supposedly had similar sightings and were also interviewed by himself and Johnson.

Thus even by 1951, this civilian group had already compiled a proper database that included an analysis that compared UFO performance with known technologies of the time. It has been made clear already that if there were bodies and craft collected from Roswell, then ATIC were fairly obviously the very last team to handle such a situation. It is also very difficult to accept that any enlisted men (bless them) such as Ruppelt would be involved in such an operation. This civilian group was obviously properly prepared and equipped for a sound investigation. They also revealed considerable experience with UFO sightings, and perhaps Johnson and Brewster provide the very faintest clue to the existence of the phantom organization referred to, an organization obviously with good communications, vehicles and resources, equipment and personnel. We have here no less than the evolution of a cultural hybrid. Fifty years later this new species of information became what we now call the New World Order.

Tribal Meet

ON MONDAY, OCTOBER 1, a tired Rosengarten and Cummings arrived at the Pentagon hot from Mitchel AFB. Having been almost without sleep for twenty four hours, they must have been trembling in their socks at the prospect of a rough meeting. Their morale must have fallen even further when they saw no less than the full array of Cabell's entire staff and a "special representative" (a civilian) from Republic Aircraft Corporation. This turns out to be none than our Mr. Brewster, and more than probably accompanied by Mr. Johnson, although he is not named in Ruppelt's published account. However, the plural is used in Ruppelt's original manuscript, so there may well have been more than one such civilian. The plural is used again by a General at the meeting, who, according to Hall and Connors (quoting Ruppelt's unpublished account), requested that the "industrial observers" leave forthwith, on account that the meeting concerned the military, who might feel compromised somewhat by their presence. However, in Ruppelt's book, he mentions that the "man from Republic" was at the meeting because of the "personal request of a general officer." We thus see the threads of disagreement between civilian and military; at this stage the hybrid culture was not yet fully unified. Ruppelt adds:

> The man from Republic supposedly represented a group of top US industrialists and scientists who thought that there should be a lot more sensible answers coming from the Air Force regarding the UFOs.

Cabell, in a bad mood and determined to put the military in their place, said that the civilians could stay, indicating their relevance and importance and relatively high intelligence compared to that on display by the military.

That civilians had access to such a meeting at all gives us an idea of the first presence of a kind of new hybrid warrior operating in the world. The military and civilian elements were becoming one and the same entity although here, as we have seen, the terms of reference are still somewhat obscure. In those days such a Man In Black techno-warrior with a foot in both camps was still largely a science fiction character. But such components of the modern world of "total" war are quite familiar to us. An example of this is the "weapons of mass destruction" propaganda, just one of a million of totally false histories woven by media and Intelligence organizations a half century after Ruppelt's time.

At this time, with the very first marketable germanium PNP transistors going into the experimental fire-control system of the prototype M-60 tank *as well as* into washing machines, an important stage of product philosophy had been reached. The weapon and the product were becoming integral parts of one another. The product itself was not the end of the process. What the product (from TV sets to cars) did was to induce a *state of mind*. This constant state of fretting mental salivation was to become the new "target," and a particular product hardly mattered after the particular state of mind to which it related had been constellated. That products, media and states of mind were related was a Postmodern idea still unborn in the head of the young Marshall McLuhan, then still at college. Looking back, we can see that this Pentagon meeting is a definitive essay in the kind of political management of concept, evidence and product that McLuhan was later to describe in *The Medium is the Message* and *Understanding Media*. As we shall see from the following analysis, this meeting gives an insight into the scaling and interpretation of perception, experience and identity within the cosmos of the military industrial complex.

If the atmosphere between the military and civilians was bad, relations within the military were worse. Cummings later told Ruppelt:

> ...all the generals and about three-fourths of the full colonels present at the meeting turned the shade of purple normally associated with rage while a sort of sickly grin graced the faces of the remaining few. Then one of the generals on the purple-faced team glared at the sickly-grin team and cut loose.[37]

The first thing this General wanted to know was who in hell had been giving him "these reports that every decent flying saucer sighting is being investigated?"

The others picked up the questioning, and there is no better picture of the kind of piecemeal confusion that reigned in the Air Force as regards the UFO. Many of these Intelligence officers offered mere chatter, tit-bits and rumour. One asked, "What happened to those two reports that General [name omitted] sent in from Saudi Arabia? He saw those two flying saucers himself."

Picking up a copy of the old Grudge Report and slamming it down on the table, another asked who released such a report, given Cabell's stated opinion that the Grudge Report "was the most poorly written, inconclusive piece of unscientific tripe"[38] that he had ever seen.

The fuming Cabell asked Cummings to give a summary of the situation as he saw it. After getting a "go ahead" glance from his chief Rosengarten, Cummings dropped his horn-rimmed spectacles to the end of his nose and spoke as only an enlisted man about to go back to civilian life could speak to a General. Obviously determined not to carry the can for the dreadful situation back at ATIC, he told all present that the whole UFO project was in complete disorder. The mass of files and reports were a completely tangled mess, beyond all hope of proper organization except by a massive effort by an experienced team of many hands.

He told how every report was taken as a huge joke. Furthermore, he accused not only Rogers, but also Colonel Watson himself, of trying to sabotage the reports by deliberately downgrading their quality. In this, he came very near to accusing Watson of cronyism. This must have struck home to an experienced man like Cabell, for such rampant cronyism as described by Cummings was a thing not exactly unheard of in Watson's generation of fighter pilots, who (just like the famed and illustrious Douglas Bader of the RAF) tended to fight alongside chums, not alongside squadrons. Cabell blew up, saying this inaction was virtually equivalent to disobeying orders. This is the greatest threat any serving officer can make, and if proved, it can lead to the gravest consequences.

At this point it must be noted that the entire discussion revolved around the analysis of reports. It was assumed rather optimistically therefore, that the "truth," whatever it turned out to be, would result from this rather academic approach of assessing paper evidence. Active field research by Air Force Intelligence officers was not even mentioned. Active field research by the civilian/scientist group represented by Mr. Brewster was probably going on night and day involving large numbers of people and covert scientific and technological resources.

But to be fair, one can see here the many difficulties the Air Force was experiencing, and perhaps many officers dug in their heels because of the formidable problems involved, rather than being particularly anti-UFO. It was supposed that Air Force men, being Air Force men, did not have the training, resources nor indeed the inclination to in-terrogate what in many cases was a civilian experience. Interrogating airmen offered much better possibilities, yes, but the trouble was that often, as regards the UFO, the civilian/military experience overlapped, and the Air Force was the last organization on Earth suitably trained to untangle the mess of mechanical imprecision and intriguing sub-jectivities this overlap often represented.

Adding to this multi-dimensional overlapping was the problem that no one knew exactly what he or she was looking for in the first place! Give this twisted bundle of experience to a sophisticated, clever scientist, then he or she might be able to take a look at such complexity, but give it to anyone of inferior mental ability, and trouble could be expected in terms of buck-passing, road-block bureaucracy, denials, and maladministration. This is a pretty standard civil service situation, and when it is mixed with the very beginnings of military-industrial conspiracy, and further mixed with politico-scientific intrigue, anything can happen, and it certainly did.

In other words, the insular collective brain of the Air Force did not have the intellectual capacity to analyze the UFO situation.

Result? Denial of everything and everything.

Thus the scene here at the Cabell meeting is an essay in power confronted by the intangible. As such, the meeting was designed for denials. Shakespeare would have loved the high-level military setting alone. What we have here is a modern techno-demonological Court of the Star Chamber, no more, no less. In addition, he would have sketched the wider background; he would also have depicted the tribal power groups, the tight ranking and status levels equivalent, certainly, to those of a mediaeval court.

Each of the eight or more full Colonels assembled here represented some vital sector of the wiring diagrams and test tubes and laboratories of young Vanguard America as she was a half century ago. These circuit diagrams of the Military Industrial cosmos are the equivalent to the old orders of angels. The different levels of denial and acceptance of mutating information can be seen here transmuting within the heads of those assembled, like a B-Feature octopus.

We have here pure American technological theatre. The rules for the actors assembled at this Air Force meeting are as tight as ever they were in any court of history or religious system, and the management of belief just as savagely applied. There is even a court Fool in the shape of the hapless Colonel Porter (the ATIC Deputy Director for "Estimates"), the anti-UFO crony of Colonel Watson. Ruppelt later described Porter as the most incompetent man in the Air Force.

The temperature rises still more. Ruppelt says that Jerry Cummings told him that the General looked at his staff of Colonels for about forty five seconds and said:

I've been lied to, and lied to, and lied to, and lied to. I want it to stop. I want the answer to the saucers and I want a good answer.

The "stupid" (Ruppelt's word) Colonel Porter in his wisdom chose this moment to say that in his opinion the UFO project was a waste of time. He got off extremely lightly, considering the temper of the General. But perhaps Porter was wise for once in choosing his moment. Cabell appears to collapse at the end of the meeting, his energy slips away from him and he goes from leader to administrator:

> The General ended up the meeting by giving a pep talk and saying that he thought that things would change…he said that he was going to keep an open mind and that he wanted the same from his staff.

Pep talk? What a pathetic note of conclusion from a man who started the two hour meeting full of tribal energy!

It was also prophetic. This was the last raging tribal meet. Within a few weeks General Samford had taken over from General Cabell and the age of bland conformist corporatism took another giant leap forward.

There would indeed be pep talks and little else from here on.

What happened to Cabell at this meeting? Well, there is a moment in Arthur Miller's play, *Death of a Salesman*, when the two sons ask their mother why their father is not acting as lively as usual. Their mother replies that their father is exhausted. The sons think she is referring to the need for a nap before dinner, but we know that she is speaking about the kind of labouring lifetime that the well fed, affluent, and over-stimulated sons will probably never experience.

By analogy, though, most at this meeting are no doubt brave and honorable men, but they are all, frankly, worn out in the deep sense that Miller meant. Almost all of them without exception had been through a terrible war, and that takes much more from men than they ever realize. As such, despite being Intelligence officers, the mental level revealed here is the level of tired railway bosses, big-store managers and supervisors. With the exception of the civilians and Ruppelt (who had a rebel streak) not a single one at the Cabell meeting has the vision or concentration or energy to apply properly to the UFO problem, still less the practical resources required.

When any military man sees that he is being out-manoeuvered, it triggers every single alarm instinct that he has. When such rising alarms occur at the same time as failing strengths, the best that he can do, like any other human being, is go through the motions of acting and thinking, and prepare for death with honor.

That is what happened at this Cabell conference.

The Air Force could not handle the UFO. It was never designed to.

Eventually, the far more clever scientists moved in and cut them out of the loop. Unfortunately in doing that, they cut out almost everybody else at the same time!

That Ruppelt did what he did in these new circumstances was a miracle never to be repeated.

There was yet another level of exhaustion present at this meeting. This level was not individually felt so much as it was a collective impression, surfacing and sinking in consciousness like a half-wrecked vessel. It was thought by most present that at last, through scientific thinking and technological application humanity, led by America, was going to write the world-script. But in this room, in this year and at this o'clock, within this fragment of Western time, the historical plots, the conspiracies and ideas, the inspirations, dreams and technologies of ten thousand and one nights are all quite stilled, their great mythological engine-heads shaking with puzzlement.

Here is the airplane and electricity meeting a bottleneck in Western Time. The plans, schemes, discoveries and experiments of Faraday, Volta, Ampere, Ohm, Helmholtz, Lodge; all the experimental clicks and buzzes of Edison, Marconi; all the abstract measuring rods and clocks of Einstein, they all flow and thread through the eye of this needle on this morning in the Pentagon.

But there is a problem. The plots have stopped. There is a stranger in town. And what a stranger! After this point, the plots of the Industrial Revolution don't fit together any more. The UFO does fit of course, but the kind of chain of being that enables it to fit is almost impossible to accept.

Postmodernism sees this as a liminal situation. The UFO is seen but it is not seen. It is there but it is not there, at one and the same time.

The great nineteenth century engineers did not have this problem. The future was theirs and theirs alone, they believed.

From the beginning of the twenty-first century, we can now look back and see the origins of the New World Order. It is like watching the assembly of a modern cathedral. But is not about Catholics, Jews, Freemasons, forms of prayer book or royal marriages any more, it is about systems: battling arrays of information, resources, technological advances all fighting for cultural primetime as once did Nell Gwynne and Greta Garbo, iconic faces now made of wires and electromagnetic pulsations.

But in 1951, future Gwynnes and Garbos were yet to arrive and find this nest fully wired up and pre-prepared for them.

Back now to Cabell, stalking the battlements like some lost soul.

A Chain of Being

The problem is that the UFO is the battlement ghost in *Hamlet*. Whenever it is in danger of being forgotten, it returns to rend minds and kingdoms, a reminder that there is something, if not rotten in the State of Denmark, then certainly most peculiar. The ghost of the murdered king has another function: as a dramatic character, it appears to be a mix of cultural reference systems. In *Hamlet* we don't know quite whether we are in a Christian universe or a Pagan one. This mix in the play leaves us as uneasy as it leaves Hamlet himself. In Cabell's universe, the analogy to this is that the liminal UFO readily swaps fact and fiction to the extent that we too do not know which Escher drawing we are in.

If the disturbed General Cabell is Hamlet the "gloomy Dane" himself, Rosenkrantz and Guildenstern are the exhausted Rosengarten and Cummings, "reeking posts" bringing news from afar to an anxious Ruppelt waiting in the wings at Wright Patterson, ready to receive news that all is not well in the kingdom.

Polanski would perhaps have directed this scene as *noir* Shakespeare with B-Feature touches. It would take place in a Faustian laboratory during the last days in the Führer bunker. Certainly the atmosphere is foul, gloomy as in Elsinore. Mysterious civilians hover in the background as an angry Cabell fumes away at his court, for all the world like the Führer himself, demanding extra efforts, reorganization, the correction of mistakes, all the things he would recommend were the matter in hand a difficult Russian strategic assessment, some new weaponry, or nuclear strategy. Polanski would have Cabell's hand jabbing at the maps and documents, yet shoot his face looking down, as if the angry General knows in his heart of hearts that, like Hamlet, he is only going through motions that are expected of him.

The Shakespearian touch is that Cabell knows that this matter in hand is very different. Perhaps he senses that, right in the middle of the young and lusty military industrial complex (the pride of America, the glamour of the world, of a then still ruined world), a stranger has appeared from another part of town. Usually they come with sheaves of paper, reports, maps, diagrams, photographs. But these strangers are different. They have nothing. Yet the stranger is there. And they needs must measure him. But where are the measurements, where is the evidence, where is the technical depth, the finite analysis, the artefacts?

There is almost nothing. To make matters worse, the investigators themselves have destroyed much of what there is, or was, of even partial measurement; how both Kafka and Borges would have relished such a situation. No, none of it makes any sense at all, yet the wretched

UFOs are still flying around. Such "damned" things, as Charles Fort called them, make Cabell and his team feel like loin cloth natives trying to describe and understand the first smoking funnel on their horizon. They have answered almost every question but this one. When this kind of special question comes along they all go into temporary shock, and their reference systems do likewise.

Polanski would have several options. He could direct Cabell as a Nero-like madman, ordering them all to stuff runner beans up their noses; he could direct Cabell himself as a frustrated rationalist, determined to get to the bottom of things, or he could portray him as a modern Hamlet, willing at one moment, baffled and puzzled the next, waiting in the wings like Ruppelt.

All image-America is here: if Cabell is Charlton Heston, the horn-rimmed Cummings is pure Art Garfunkel Ivy League cool. Rosengarten is the Jewish intellectual loaded with theory, the technological equivalent to the Hassidic theology of old. Who controls the world? A half century later we still do not know.

Perhaps, as Charles Fort said, "we are property."

Who owns us?

Nothing more mysterious than images. They are what own us — lock, stock and barrel.

BUT THE AIR FORCE men present here would have no such solution. There is anger, bitterness and frustration. The UFO is in action again, and again no one knows what to do. Again, these are iron men with decorations from WWII four inches thick on their chest. They would have no problem with any single thing concrete, measurable, finite, continuous and tangible. Yet this phenomenon is confusing them.

Such confusion is a very special and most unusual thing in this techno-military context. Differing levels of technical competence, concentration, and mental ability are impossible to focus into unity. The problem can't be objectified. As in an Escher-Penrose drawing, there is a cerebral component missing. The tribal terms of reference are not sufficient. They try to modify the tribal systems of reference just as pointer readings of instrumentation may indeed be modified, improved by a molecular process of mathematics and experimentation.

There is a problem. Cultural growth (and science and the MIC are very much cultures in change, growth and decay) is determined by the quantity and quality of the problems posed by the need for survival and development both. There can be a long period of time when the management of the problem-solving apparatus appears to be successful. Crisis is always brought about by the almost determined appearance of a particular problem that the cultural tools cannot deal with. At first this special kind of problem looks as if it is merely a more complex and difficult extension of preceding problems. But it is not. This problem means that the very world-view itself has to change. Engineering and new problem management techniques won't solve this special problem.

If this special problem is not solved, then the culture, as well as the individuals concerned, goes into shock.

The men at this meeting know it is not the Russians, they know it is not pilot hallucination, and they know it is not the planet Venus nor swamp gas that experienced fighter pilots are reporting. Here at this meeting, we have men looking for engineering solutions and not realizing that they have a world-view change on their hands. The only thing known is the engineering solution. Whilst these can tackle almost any and every human problem, they cannot tackle the UFO. The idea of world-view change is, with great respect to these men, above their intellect. They are Warriors, not intellectuals.

No wonder the Air Force got rid of the UFO in 1969, and closed down Operation Blue Book forever. It was not because it was a false or true thing, a real or unreal thing, but because it was quite beyond their capacity in any respect to handle. They admitted its existence implicitly by saying that since the airborne phenomenon did not appear to be hostile, then it was not the concern of the United States Air Force.

When History finally examines and judges this statement, it will be looked upon as one of the most disreputable and cowardly get-outs of all time.

From Cabell onwards, the final development of the corporate stage is the adaptation of a philosophy of denial. Just as the Right was to deny the Holocaust, and the Left the camps of the Gulag Archipelago, the United States Air Force was to deny the UFO an existence. Ruppelt was left to wander for a brief time, but on such a shortening leash that by the time he left the Air Force in late 1951, Project Blue Book was again down to a two-man operation.

The meeting closes.

Rosengarten and Cummings now return to Dayton.

With Cummings going back to civilian life, Ruppelt is put in charge of what was left of the shortening life of Project Grudge, now briefly referred to as New Project Grudge.

A Set of
Correspondences

The Corporation Man Cometh

NEW PROJECT GRUDGE WITH RUPPELT IN CHARGE WAS
officially established on October 27, 1951. Ruppelt was in an up-beat
mood, quite excited and ready to go. He was now very much the captain
of his own ship, and relaxed and confident enough to regard even the
bureaucracy involved with mild sarcasm, as distinct from heavy:

> I'd written the necessary letters and received the necessary en-
> dorsements. I'd estimated, itemized, and justified direct costs and
> manpower. I'd conferred, and referred, and now I had the money to
> operate.[1]

Few military men have this kind of combination of enthusiasm,
organizational power, and the ability to laugh at themselves as well as
others. He continues: "The next step was to pile up all this paper work
as an aerial barrier, let the saucers crash into it, and fall just outside
the door." Obviously, as far as energy and all-round ability were concerned, Lieutenant-Colonel Rosengarten had picked a winner.

However, Ruppelt did not avoid what media folk today sometimes
call "liberal burn."[2] This means that a situation can be so finely
balanced between opposing views that any meaningful results are
cancelled out. This rather weak hesitancy reveals itself in quite a few
of his more difficult investigations, and the frequent shrugging of his
shoulders is at times embarrassing. On occasion he reveals something
of the timid bureaucrat in him. If he had chosen the Air Force as a
career and had attended intensive staff courses, instructors would
have flayed him alive for this kind of easy-going indecision and what
amounts at times to a washing of hands. Above all other things, a
military man must be capable of making a decision one way or another,
and more often than not that does not include retreat. A leader who

hesitates in battle is a dead man.

He pursued this "liberal burn" policy to a fault in forming the basic policy of his organization:

> If anyone became anti-flying saucer and was no longer capable of making an unbiased evaluation of a report, out he went. Conversely anyone who became a believer was through. We were too busy during the initial phases of the project to speculate as to whether the unknowns were spaceships, space monsters, Soviet weapons, or ethereal visions.[3]

He adds that he had to sack three members of his New Grudge staff "for being too pro or too con."

This might not have been the most exciting of policies, but at least it was a good diplomatic move. The higher military echelon liked what they saw happening, if only because it meant that often nothing happened at all. However Ruppelt, the good scout as he ever was, did his best. Colonel Frank Dunn the new Chief of ATIC took to Ruppelt's idea of giving UFO briefings to the wide spectrum of visiting technical consultants to ATIC. For the first two weeks at least following the birth of New Grudge, every "scientist, engineer, or scholar" who visited ATIC was given a UFO briefing. Ruppelt was unable to name these people (it would be nice to know the names of the scholars at least!) but says that a list of their names would read "like a page from *Great Men of Science.*" Given this high rating it is reasonable to assume that the names on this list would include some members of the original MJ-12 group. It can be seen also that here we have the proper foundation of what might be called a UFO-investigation culture founded, moreover, on a broad scientific and technological base, although the same conformist filter applied to this as to all scientific studies. The assumption that nature is a good, honest, hard working Protestant bourgeois that lies supine to be "investigated" is reflected in the structure of a psychosocial filter. A good intelligence agent would smile at this as a method of procedure. Ruppelt is already framing the answers he wants to the shape of the investigation he wants. Perhaps an alien would know exactly what a good agent knows: look as if you are absolutely nobody and you become almost invisible; this done, our possible alien can slip through the statistical significances and go and do anything he, she, or it wants to do.

Be this as it may, once in charge Ruppelt started effectively rebuilding the old Project Grudge. He consulted and briefed many of the high powered scientific and technical experts who visited ATIC to give advice, instruction, and information on a wide range of more conventional matters. His description of the happy and exciting co-operative atmosphere at ATIC in 1951 shows how times have changed since then: "I found that UFO's [sic] were being freely and seriously discussed in scientific circles." He took a straw poll of such visitors to his Project Grudge office at Wright-Patterson, and was most surprised by the result. Of nine visitors, "two thought the Air Force was wasting its time, one could be called indifferent, and six were very enthusiastic." Though the following is a significant snap statistic, it gives some indication of the state of affairs regarding the UFO within the senior scientific and military professions in 1951:

> Every one of the nine scientists and engineers who had reviewed the UFO material at ATIC had made one strong point: we should give strong priority to getting reasonably accurate measurements of the speed, altitude, and size of reported UFOs.[4]

In other words, once some part of the UFO could be got into the objective Cartesian frame, the project would be getting somewhere.

Two weeks before Christmas, 1951, Ruppelt and the Chief of ATIC, Colonel Dunn, were summoned to the Pentagon to report on the progress of the revitalization of Project Grudge. By this time Major General John A. Samford had replaced Major General Cabell as Director of Air Force Intelligence. This meeting went a lot more smoothly than the previous meeting with Cabell. The encouraging atmosphere impressed Ruppelt. The calm, diplomatic Samford had been briefed previously on UFO matters. Little did Ruppelt guess that this atmosphere was as phoney as silicon tits, and that eventually, as we shall see, the cool General was going to sell our hero right down the cool corporation river.

But not just yet.

Colonel Dunn briefed the company on what the New Project Grudge had achieved, emphasizing particularly the high quality of the scientific liaison established by Ruppelt. General W.M. Garland, General Samford's Assistant for Production, then stated that it had been decided that the Air Force was to be the responsible agency for all UFO reports and analysis.

Ruppelt then gave his report.

As a definite attention-raiser, he started off by discussing how important the situation was by showing the attention of UFOs to strategic areas of the United States:

UFOs were seen more frequently around areas vital to the defence of the United States. The Los-Alamos-Albuquerque area, Oak Ridge, and the White Sands Proving Ground rated high. Port areas, Strategic Air Command Bases, and industrial areas ranked next. UFO's [sic] had been reported in every state in the Union and from every foreign country. The US did not have a monopoly.[5]

He talked also to the meeting about media relations and policy. In doing this, he showed that he was now getting just a little wary of media as a component in the process of social cognition. But typical of many in those days, he thought he could control the very young, hungry monster by the application of a few commonsense, honest-to-goodness techniques. He explained to the Samford meeting:

> I felt sure that before long the press would get wind of the Air Force's renewed effort to identify UFOs. When this happened, instead of being mysterious about the whole thing, we would freely admit the existence of the new project, explain the situation thoroughly and exactly as it was, and say that all UFO reports made to the Air Force would be given careful consideration. In this way we would encourage more people to report what they were seeing and we might get some good data.[6]

We really must not be cynical about such blushing naïveté. Ruppelt was a very nice man, but here he is out of his depth, and unaware (as were many) that media would grow into a new Estate entirely, whose power and influence would grow to challenge every single sector of politics, society and moral authority. Very few knew in 1951 that not only would media grow beyond all social control, it would become a virtual information-animal with its own complex of agendas. Even fewer knew that Fact was not going to work in television, it being a non-cerebral medium that worked on images. In Ruppelt's time, images were still things in art studios; that they were to escape from there to rule the world as a powerful new Estate was not forecast. Radios were as big as small suitcases; they still had hot glowing valves, and most needed stout shelves to stand on. To this day, many souls still do not understand this planetary takeover by an information-form, and we could not expect Ruppelt to have understood such a thing fifty years ago. Like most people of his time, he thought that media was a semi-passive entity that merely reflected circumstances and obeyed fairly simple laws. His was a fairly typical view of media relations for his time. Information had not yet become performance art. There were still differential mechanical relations between input and output, although they were starting to become a little uncertain:

> The UFO reports had never stopped coming since they had first started in June 1947. There was some correlation between publicity and the number of sightings, but it was not an established fact that reports came in only when the press was playing UFOs. Just within the past few months the number of good reports had increased sharply and there had been no publicity.[7]

Thus at this time it was universally accepted that "media" could be separated out from what was assumed to be a fairly simple external truth of "facts." Given this shaky assumption, with a little thought, truth could be very easily separated from fiction, and media "impressions" properly corrected.

All human groups without exception are governed by symbols and types, role-playing and staged events. Ruppelt here is behaving like a character that has just stepped out of a Norman Rockwell painting. Here his role is that of the bright honest village boy with a spanner, familiar from wartime posters. His pigeon chest swells with pride as he fights the corrupt guile of the syndicate and "false" media "impressions."

In this respect, Ruppelt had all the limitations of the thoroughgoing practical military scientists of his time. Brilliant as they might be, most were village boys trying to clean up the world with their brand-new shining tools. Massive environmental damage, the failure of nuclear power, and the intellectual shame of animal experimentation, to name but three Faustian disasters — none of these things had yet fully arrived in 1951.

Neither could Ruppelt be expected to cope with an emerging post-industrial situation in which, when some beloved vectors of "measurement" are duly produced, they are promptly denied at one and the same time. Fifty years later, every significant news headline contains evidence of monumental duplicity and corruption. As these words are typed, in comes news of the mysterious death of a British bio-weapons inspector.

Of course he will have acted alone.

As with JFK, and the death of Diana, there will no conspiracy.

AS DISTINCT FROM seeing media as an active blurring of such hard distinctions, Ruppelt saw media as passive: it was as friendly as a manual typewriter and the family dog and, given just a bit of common sense, it could be controlled almost as completely. The outline of his media policy as given at this Pentagon meeting is therefore somewhat horse and cart, very definitely a thing of pre-JFK complexity, to say the least. Ruppelt did not live to see the post-JFK world and its fall to Vietnam and Watergate. After JFK was gone, the American experience of received "reality" was to become something much more complex than a simple direct relationship between the observer and what was observed.

History consists of these tree-rings. They measure time not in hours or years, but in terms of evolving experience. Ruppelt is such a tree-ring. He was perhaps one of the last great American innocents in that respect, and that is why his work and personality are worthy of study. He lived, worked and thought in the last historical hours of happy, practical school-lab science and its boyish innocence that assumed that truth (paradoxically, just like the hated Communist posters of the time) could be reached by hard work and application. Through reason, by the finding of "objective" fact, and rational experimentation, the honest worker could achieve freedom from the artificially wrought "mystifications" of his cruel and fiendishly clever exploiters. In this respect science, communism and bourgeois capitalism all share the same mythology.

But despite the mighty efforts of hopeful social-democratic theorists, and the visionaries of positive social-scientific democracy, after Ruppelt the entire military industrial complex and corporate science in the West were steadily to become devious, hidden, paranoid entities. Fifty years on from Ruppelt, they have become indeed those dark forms prophesied by all the earliest flying saucer visionaries, from George Adamski to John Keel. In this respect the "rejected" experience of the UFO contactees tells us more about the subtexts than do social historians of the conventional variety. The scientist himself, regarded by Ruppelt with an almost blushing, boy scout enthusiasm is now, culturally speaking, almost a devil figure. One would be hard pressed trying to find in any media at all a positive view of science and scientists. Within both the B-Feature and the popular imagination at large, they are always seen as dark, almost satanic figures of governmental authority and corporate conspiracy.

The Report on Unidentified Flying Objects is therefore not only a superb essay on time and threat, culture and weapons, it is a picture of the fall from grace of post-war America and its sunny but treacherous scientific hopes. Already this second Pentagon meeting differs from the first, held only a few months previously. The tribal primitivism has gone, the tempers, and the conflicts; here we have the birth of the Cool represented by the cerebral General Samford who, as distinct from

Cabell, would think several times before aiming a punch to the jaw.[8]

Little did Ruppelt know it, but Samford was a sign that the goal posts were being changed. If he had seen them being changed, he would have reached the rather disappointing conclusion that whatever the universe was about, it was not about honest hard work and good behaviour. Contrary to popular belief, the corporation always has a most unstable relationship with clever people. As a live body of information, it has its own agendas that clever folk may or may not fit into. Clever-clever folk can be dealt with by promoting them out of existence, but people who are far too clever for their own good often disappear in mysterious circumstances. Hundreds of defence research scientists have disappeared without trace over the past thirty years, and not always due to enemy action, thus giving a new meaning to the phrase "friendly fire."

Another disadvantage Ruppelt had was that he didn't belong to the Club. He was not a regular airman; he was not Ivy League, or a graduate from an American Military Academy. He had not been through a Staff Course, and he did not come from a moneyed and privileged background that higher ranks came from at this time. Neither was he a serving drone or mechanic; he had brains and personality, both deadly curses within any corporation.

Thus was Ruppelt hobbled. In this author's opinion, it was not beyond the wit of his superiors to make the prediction that when he again became a civilian, this able man would write a book about his experiences as an insider; he might have discussed this in passing, it might have been a mere remark or a phone call, buried in the noise of the day. But the corporation, like a religious body (which it is, of course) has many ways of sorting out signals from noise, and such a tiny mistake would have made its way up the ladder very quickly.

Another signal that might well have been detected was Ruppelt's increasing resentment towards the Air Force and its handling of the UFO situation. This expression gathers momentum throughout every chapter of *The Report on Unidentified Flying Objects,* and it bursts out in full, turning to bitterness after the UFO sightings at Washington National Airport. In this respect, it must have been obvious that at no time did Ruppelt feel he was the complete professional airman, and as always in the armed forces, there is always a great barrier between the professional and the enlisted cadre.

Again, perhaps when you take a man's second youth as well as his first, he can no longer be relied upon as a friend. And perhaps Ruppelt learned something else. That truth and reality related to style, with intellect coming way down the promotional ladder of the gods. This is the point where the Protestant "hard word and application equals truth and reality" equations break down.

The irony is that later in his life, as we shall see, he was forced to change the goal posts himself, like any good corporation man. But by that time he had become a veteran at this game, and took good care to leave signs before he died, that the changes he was forced to make to the goal posts were false changes, to be read by later generations as a code which, when cracked, would reveal all was not well. He tried to stay an honest mechanic, but at the end perhaps he broke out.

We shall pick up on these signals from the grave later in this book.

But corporate manoeuvres notwithstanding, by comparison to our own time the open-mindedness revealed at this Pentagon meeting, at least, appears to be impressive. Ruppelt was pleased. Everyone at the meeting had been properly briefed on UFO matters, and two admitted there and then that they had seen UFOs. One of these was Brigadier General William M. Garland, described by Ruppelt as a "moderately confirmed believer." Garland claimed that he had seen a UFO whilst stationed at Sacramento in 1950.

Everyone present agreed with Ruppelt's approach. Using a blackboard (probably the very last one in the Pentagon!) he explained an analytical technique quite as lost as the blackboard. Forms should be designed said he, and if a UFO is seen by large numbers of people, then "it would be profitable for us to go out and talk to these people," ask them to fill in the form, and find out

> the time they saw the UFO, and where they saw it (the direction and height above the horizon). Then we might be able to use these data, work out a triangulation problem, and get a fairly accurate measurement of speed, altitude, and size.[9]

Vintage America here again! The idea of uniformed Air Force Officers (presumably all home-town Dick Tracy lookalikes!) requesting good folk and true to fill in forms about their UFO sightings is an idea from the Last Days of American innocence.

Maybe it was a Spaceship

A FEW DAYS LATER, back at ATIC, Ruppelt got the green light from the Pentagon. He had already written up a staff study, and sent it to the Pentagon for approval. One of the main points he made in this plan was that New Project Grudge would need a proper staffing level. He would need advice and analysis from an astronomer, a chemist, a mathematician, a psychologist and "probably a dozen other specialists." This shows Ruppelt at his best. At this time such a multi-disciplinary view as he proposed, particularly concerning a civilian/military enterprise, was unheard of. Even Air Force cooking and laundry were carried out on a hire and fire basis by individuals. In 1951, what were then called Time and Motion Studies were only just arriving in the Air Force. Although the Office of Naval Research had sponsored a computer course at the Moore School in 1946, the first stored-programme computer (EDVAC, based on von Neumann architecture) was not completed until 1952.[10] At this time Robert "systems analysis" MacNamara, the later Secretary of State for Defense, was still at college, with his brilliantly conceived critical-path analysis and cost/effective plans (unfortunately to prove disastrous in Vietnam) still in his ambitious head.

The very day after Christmas Day, 1951 (he was a regular working beaver, was our captain!) Ruppelt left Dayton with Colonel S.H. Kirkland of Colonel Dunn's staff for a two day conference with an organization that at the time he could not name because of its secret work. We know now that this was the Battelle Institute. Again, we see the military/civilian seam cross-fertilizing, but his idea was impressive by Air Force standards. The object was to commission Project Bear (as Ruppelt called his proposal) to organize and sub-contract scientific, social and psychological research studies, where relevant, to all UFO matters. The psychological angle concerned the design of a form to be filled in by anyone who claimed a UFO sighting. The form looked simple enough, but really it was a paper version of a hidden lie-detector test to establish mental consistency, space-time concept stability, and to detect implicit emphasis in statements and observations.

It all sounds innocent enough. But again, we see the military/civilian seam quite clearly expressed by a condescending, almost Pavlovian elitism. Then, as now, it was assumed that the general public are confused and simple-minded creatures; they are devious and unintelligent in turn; their IQ is low, their basic education is unsound and, as judges of that precious concept called reality, they are never ever to be trusted.

Of course, as a good way of wiping out an experience and intimidating a confused and uncertain observer this form was absolutely perfect. But after 1951, in every major Western country, this kind of highly dangerous psychosocial testing was to proliferate and indeed become an important measure of social-scientific reality.

A Set of Correspondences

THE SECOND STUDY to be undertaken by Batelle was quite different. This was a proposal for a statistical analysis of, initially at least, a collection of some 650 UFO reports, perhaps with many thousands more to come. This proposal shows Ruppelt in his true creative element. In those days, the word "computer" had hardly arrived and neither had solid-state memory, but nevertheless, punch card techniques were quite effective, if slow. The military were just beginning to take an interest in civilian and police pioneered techniques concerning analysis of sales, distribution and manufacturing in the first case, and criminal records in the second. Ruppelt called the IBM computer used by Battelle a "card-sorting machine," and 100 items pertaining to a UFO report would be put on each card. As an act of early technological symbiosis, the items punched on the cards would correspond to the items on the questionnaires that Project Bear was going to develop. As an early example of software thinking from a non-specialist, applied to an out-of-the-box subject, this work was not bad at all; in fact it was well-nigh bloody heroic (if not downright revolutionary) as regards the stick-in-the-mud Air Force.

Unfortunately this daring experiment, whilst it made keeping records and finding information much easer, fell down on the correlation expectations which eventually proved, like the UFO manifestation itself, to be disappointingly vague.

A few days later Ruppelt was on his way to the Air Defence Command Headquarters in Colorado Springs. Again he was made welcome, given a thorough briefing, and a "promise that they would do anything they could to help solve the UFO riddle." Given that he had received dire warnings that most doors would be shut to him as the official ATIC UFO officer, Ruppelt found this cooperative atmosphere most surprising, and comments, "I was becoming aware that there was much wider concern about UFO reports than I'd ever realized before."[11]

UFO reports were coming in all the time, but in the manner of trusting only experienced observers, Ruppelt paid a lot of attention to the balloon experts of the Aeronautical Division of General Mills Incorporated. This firm did any and every kind of balloon work for the civilian and military sectors, using both manned and unmanned balloons. They launched the big skyhook balloons that took a whole range of equipment up to the fringes of space, and the observers in the manned variety were rated amongst the best in the world. Unlike jet pilots, these men spent many hours in their tiny gondolas and capsules, often moving at a very slow speed, and sometimes were almost stationary in the sky for long periods observing weather changes, recording pressure, humidity, temperature changes and cloud conditions. They also operated equipment that could record anything from cosmic radiation to sunbursts, and they used many different types of camera.

Their UFO reports had been sent to New Grudge because they had heard the Project was being re-organized under Ruppelt — having had an unsatisfactory reception from previous staff. Our man spent a whole day talking to the balloon crews and Mills technical staff and, knowing the reputation of these men as observers of things in the sky, he was quite astonished at the reports. The experienced Mills crews, familiar with all kinds of sky lighting and atmospheric conditions, meteorology, aerodynamics and astronomy, said they saw so many UFOs they had long since ceased taking any notice of them.

Ruppelt has space to give details of one significant case only. On January 16, 1951, two staff from General Mills and four others from Artesia, New Mexico, were watching a skyhook balloon from Artesia airport. After an hour of observation they saw two tiny specks appear on the horizon. The two specks began to move fast towards the observers, to reveal themselves as round, dull-white objects flying in close formation. When these objects reached the balloon they circled it once and tipped on edge, revealing disc-shaped bodies. They then flew off to the northwest, soon disappearing into the far horizon. If they had been near the balloon as estimated, they would have been about sixty feet in diameter.

Another interesting sighting at this time occurred on the morning of January 21, 1952. A Navy pilot had taken off from Mitchel Air Force Base, New York in a Grumman TBM (torpedo bomber) Avenger. He was an experienced lieutenant commander with WWII experience, and he was somewhat surprised to see an anomalous object shaped like a parachute top circling the airfield at about 2,500 feet. The object began a gradual climb, and the pilot followed the climb, staying above and off to the right of the object. The UFO started a left turn, the pilot tried to cut inside this turn, but he overshot and passed over the object, which started to gain speed. In seconds, the UFO made a quite astonishing 180° turn, accelerating rapidly as it did so, and finally left the poor propeller-driven TBM struggling hopelessly in attempted pursuit.

The tower had told the pilot that a balloon had been launched, but neither the TBM flight track nor the UFO's manoeuvres could possibly match the measured balloon flight, although both Ruppelt and the pilot tried hard to produce a balloon explanation. The dome-shaped object was white on top with a dark underside, and the main evidence against its being a balloon was that it pulled away from the TBM as the pilot followed it for a minute at full speed.

This incident was typical of many UFO/pilot experiences of the time. The most hair-raising aspect of many of such incidents (which continue in full spate fifty years later) is that the objects, whatever they are, suggest that somehow they are aware of such pursuits, and indeed casually draw away from their pursuers in a most measured manner, increasing speed steadily and performing extraordinary manoeuvres quite beyond the technology of the present day, never mind half a century ago.

What could Ruppelt say or do in the face of such plain evidence of an utterly fantastic event? He gets out of it quite gracefully by letting the pilot speak for himself:

> I don't know what it was, but I've never seen anything like it before or since — maybe it was a spaceship.

Ruppelt's response to this ends chapter nine of *The Report on Unidentified Flying Objects*:

> I went back to Dayton stumped — maybe it was a spaceship.

We have to consider here just what a massive blow to the ego the presence of such manifestations represents. For a moment the "advanced" culture that built the TBM faced the possibility of living alongside (as distinct from being invaded by) a culture whose nature is almost inconceivable. When we realize that this culture may well have exactly the same problems with another level "above" itself, we can begin to understand the psychology of sceptical blindness to such events, and see organized militant scepticism as a control. This is essential to the scaling down and attempted vanishing of experiences that are difficult to manage. Without such a control we might, like the Australian aboriginals and the cargo worshippers of the Solomon Islands, just go into cultural shock when we realize that the culture above us is just as complex and multifarious as is the culture below.

The Lab Was Never Heard From Again

THE PACE OF EVENTS faced by the harassed Ruppelt in early 1952 was quickening. Only some twenty minutes after midnight on January 22, there occurred a peculiar incident at one of the most northern radar outposts in Alaska.

At 0020 hours, a bright distinct spot appeared on a radarscope.

This target was located over one of the most remote and desolate regions of the world, a region that saw almost no aircraft at all apart from rare military flights. No less than three good plots of this target showed that it was a solid object at 23,000 feet and travelling at 1,500 mph, no less! Such a speed in 1951 was quite impossible for any known aircraft design. The aerodynamic problems presented by such a speed were to take at least another fifteen years of quite intense scientific and technological research to solve.

The duty controller, an Air Force Captain, seeing the rapid trail of dots across the scope that meant the 1,500 mph object was only some fifty miles away from the base, quickly scrambled an F-94 fighter from a base 100 miles away. Within a very short time both the F-94 and the object were on the scope when a most peculiar thing happened. The UFO, as if detecting the F-94, slowed down rapidly, stopped, and then reversed its course before the wide eyes of the operators! With the object closing on the station, the set was switched to short-range and it promptly lost both the object and the F-94.

With the first F-94 going back to base because of lack of fuel, a second F-94 was scrambled, and the radar switched back to long range, thus locating both the UFO and the second F-94, which was vectored towards the UFO. With both targets again closing in on the station, the aerials were switched to short range again, and again lost both objects. Suddenly the F-94 radar operator reported a weak return off to his right at 28,000 feet. Climbing towards the calculated position of the return, the UFO faded away, but swinging the F-94 round for another pass, the radar operator reported a strong return. But this time, unbelievably, the target was scarcely moving! The object was again picked up by ground radar, but the second F-94 had to return to base.

Yet a third F-94 was scrambled. After a ten minute search, they were over the station itself when the airborne radar operator reported that he had a strong return. But again, the ground radar on short range could not locate either the aircraft or the UFO, both being so near the station and the "dead" area of the station's transmissions. In what must have been a thrilling moment for the two-man crew, the F-94 came within some 200 estimated yards of the UFO, the pilot pulling rapidly up lest he collide with the object. Here is Ruppelt's own description of this incredible event:

> He made another pass and another, but each time the bright spot
> on the radar operator's scope just stayed in one spot as if something
> were defiantly sitting out in front of the F-94 daring the pilot to close

in. The pilot didn't take the dare. On each pass he broke off at 200 yards.[12]

Let us just take in the meaning of this situation as reported. Alone, the reduction of a speed of 1,500 mph to almost stationary was in those days in the realms of science fiction, and remains there a half century later. This rate of deceleration and the ability nonchalantly to hover at thousands of feet in the freezing skies of Alaska represents some technology quite inconceivable to us. That no aerofoil shape was ever seen visually by the F-94 crew compounds the problem. Whoever or whatever was guiding the object obviously had no problem with the possible knowledge that the F-94 interceptors were on active duty. They were also armed with 50-cal machine-guns, which at 200 feet might have given some UFOnauts at least an interesting moment or two.

The decision of ATIC on this event? It was due to freak weather! Captain James, chief of the radar section at ATIC, persuaded Ruppelt at the time that this was the explanation. Yet, Ruppelt adds, it was a clear moonlit night, and to add to the mystery, the crews of the interceptors had not seen a thing!

In these early months of 1952, reports of radar sightings increased rapidly, most of these reports coming from the Air Defence Command. Soon after the Alaskan incident Ruppelt got a telephone call from the chief of one of the sections of a civilian experimental radar laboratory in New York State. Ruppelt's caller said, "Some damn odd things are happening that are beginning to worry me." The lab technicians had checked everything they could think of, but still they were getting many anomalous returns of such scope definition and such performance peculiarity that they thought that the Air Force ought to be informed as soon as possible. Ruppelt, in a rather limp moment, told them to send in a report by mail to ATIC.

The report duly arrived, hand-carried by no less than a General from Headquarters, Air Material Command. He had been at the radar laboratory and, hearing of these events, had offered personally to deliver the report to Wright-Patterson. Since the report concerned radar, Ruppelt was obliged to give the report to ATIC's electronics branch, where unfortunately it fell into the hands of the old anti-UFO veterans of the previous Projects Sign and Grudge. He tells us that the head of the Electronics Branch lectured the head of the laboratory (a man who possibly wrote the textbooks the staff of the Electronics Branch had used in college) all about how a weather inversion can cause false targets. He was gracious enough to tell the chief of the radar lab to call if he had any more "trouble."

The lab was never heard from again.

This kind of event made Ruppelt even more determined to improve relations with Air Defence Command Headquarters. He travelled to Colorado Springs in early February with a definite plan of how ADC could assist ATIC in getting better data on UFOs. Again, meeting the higher intelligence of the bigger boys, he made much better progress than with the lower-case, garage-limited elements of ATIC. In contrast, for a middle ranking Air Force enlisted officer, he was received like royalty:

> I briefed General Benjamin W. Chidlaw, then the Commanding General of the Air Defence Command, and his staff, telling them about our plan. They agreed with it in principle and suggested that I work out the details with the Director of Intelligence for the ADC, Brigadier W.M. Burgess. General Burgess designated Major Verne Sadowski of his staff to be the ADC liaison officer with New Grudge.[13]

What an open society America was then! Here is Ruppelt giving dates, times, places, individual ranks, personalities, plus departmental functions and operational assignments. In our own time no ex-officer would be allowed to write such details. Over a half century, this closing down of communication between major sectors of society was to cost America dear. One sees a technological tragedy: a vanishing by technology of all the traditional processes involved in the recognition of values and identity within the social fabric.

The result of Ruppelt's visit was that ADC issued a directive to all their units explaining the UFO situation and how to take appropriate action. All radar units equipped with scope cameras would be required to take photographs of targets that the operators considered to be in the UFO category. Such photos, along with a completed questionnaire, would be forwarded to New Grudge. The Ground Observer Corps would be integrated into the UFO reporting net, and individual controllers had the option to scramble fighters when quite anomalous, definite and bright returns were registered.

The International Brigade

IN THIS SAME MONTH of February, 1952, the Canadians came into the picture. Two Royal Canadian Air Force officers visited Ruppelt and told him they were getting their share of UFO reports. Their visit had been prompted by an incident at North Bay, Ontario, about 200 miles north of Buffalo, New York. Looking back from the time of publication of his book in 1956, Ruppelt describes many such contacts during his time at New Grudge and Blue Book, and gives some idea of the high-level of worldwide UFO interest at this time. He says that "the visitors who passed through my office closely resembled the international brigade." And here is the covert way it all worked:

> Most of the visits were unofficial in the sense that the officers came to ATIC on other business, but in many other instances the other business was just an excuse to come out to Dayton to get filled in on the UFO story.[14]

And many things come right out of the bag:

> Two RAF intelligence officers who were in the US on a classified mission brought six single-space typed pages of questions they and their friends wanted answered.[15]

Months later, Ruppelt was to let out two more intriguing tit-bits about the RAF. In discussing the Operation Mainbrace sightings and the sightings over Topcliffe Aerodrome (this last word was still just current at the time), he says, "It was these sightings, I was told by an RAF exchange intelligence officer in the Pentagon, that caused the RAF to officially recognize the UFO."[16]

The amount of interest in the UFO was therefore worldwide, and the level of active dissemination of what technical information was available was somewhat energetic, if only in the hope that some scientist or researcher somewhere would come up with something. It is of note, of course, that this open-mindedness was strictly limited to a specialized elite. In no way did the free sharing of information take place in the public or the media domain. The public could simply be ignored and the media, not yet nearly as dangerous as it was to become fifty years later, could be left to play its simple-minded entertaining doll-games for the peasantry. The elite didn't even have to close their doors, as it were, because exits and entrances hardly existed in any case in the sealed world of 1950s mandarins so well described in C.P. Snow's novels. It is a pity that the astute Snow didn't catch Ruppelt's book when it was first published. For instance, Ruppelt tells us about constant in-depth briefings with the "international brigade":

> To get the word to the other countries, we enlisted the gratis aid

of scientists who were planning to attend conferences or meetings in Europe. We would brief these European-bound scientists on all aspects of the UFO problem, so they could informally discuss the problem with their European colleagues.[17]

The level of enthusiasm for UFO research amongst folk not known for enthusiasms surprised Ruppelt frequently. As soon as the date and time of a Blue Book briefing was announced in the various bulletins available to those with the proper security clearances, there was not a seat left in the house. Often he would arrive at a laboratory or research establishment to find that the briefing had not been squeezed in merely between more important matters, but given a whole day to ensure a good in-depth session. He did note, however, that there was a considerable difference between what the scientists said to the press (Ruppelt hardly mentions TV — its flickering grainy screen was only a small presence in his day), and what they said in private. This was to become a growing practice as the mid-century moved on, and many of Jacques Vallee's "secret colleges" of science and technology were formed at this time. The open-minded, pre-war "democratic" scientists such as Arthur Eddington and those pioneers of the idea of "scientific education," such as Karl Pearson and Lancelot Hogben, would have been horrified at this development of closed circuit specialisations within the impenetrable cells of the secretly financed corporate conspiracies.

Here *The Report on Unidentified Flying Objects* is doubly valuable in that it describes, no less, the very beginning of what we now call the New World Order, which was the birth of a new cosmos entirely. When we read passages such as the following, we begin to take the ideas of Stanton Friedman, Kevin Randle and the Woods about MJ-12 more seriously:

> Colonel S.H. Kirkland and I once spent a whole day briefing and talking to the Beacon Hill Group, the code name for a collection of some of the world's leading scientists and industrialists. This group, formed to consider and analyze the toughest of military problems, took a very serious interest in our project and gave much good advice. At Los Alamos and again at Sandia Base our briefings were given in auditoriums to standing room only crowds. In addition I gave my briefings at National Advisory Committee for Aeronautics laboratories, at Air Research and Development centres, at Office of Naval Research facilities and at the Air Force University.[18]

Blue Book is Go

BY MARCH 1952, New Grudge, because of the increasing number of sightings, had become a project within ATIC quite separate from all others. It was therefore re-named Project Blue Book and given a much higher status within ATIC. This meant more staff and proper independent funding, since other projects unconnected to UFOs had in the past resented siphoning off some their money allotment to New Grudge, which was regarded as something of an Orphan Annie within ATIC. The average number of sightings had increased from about ten a month to twenty a month since December 1951. By March 1952, the reports had dropped off a little, but in April, Project Blue Book received no less than ninety nine reports.

Ruppelt announces the new Project with a proud description of dynamic power and efficiency. He says he had

> ten people on my regular staff plus many paid consultants representing every field of science. All of us on Project Blue Book had Top Secret security clearances so that security was no block in our investigations. Behind this organization was a reporting network made up of every Air Force base intelligence officer and every Air Force radar station in the world, and in the Air Defence Command's Ground Observer Corps.[19]

But in practice, the picture was very different. Both human beings and organizations were, as always, in a mess. Though Ruppelt sounds in a good mood from the above, his book is a constant stream of bursts of sarcasm and anger against the Air Force policy on UFOs. This rage increases throughout the book until it reaches crescendo after the Washington National Airport sightings. The anti-UFO Colonel Watson was now gone officially,[20] and replaced by the much more sympathetic Colonel Frank Dunn, but there were still personality clashes within ATIC. The Radar group in particular gave Ruppelt many problems. But at least the Air Force had, for the first time, a properly constituted UFO investigation body under the command of a very capable officer.

From its very beginning, Project Blue Book was being asked increasingly for information and cooperation by interested parties from other countries. The UFO was become a common transnational experience, and emerging psychosocial theories that UFO sightings were the result of hysteria and the effect of American popular culture were as laughable then as they are today. Ruppelt was not exactly surprised to find that the investigators who contacted him had their own indigenous military/civilian UFO research groups that operated their own covert/overt activity sectors. This often murky cultural cross-fertilization was later to breed many hybrid forms of role and organization, purpose and motivation. From Ruppelt's time onwards people were to discover very quickly that both media in general and the great corporate "information society" in particular were often quite unable (or unwilling) to give any information about anything at all.

In a web age, conspiracy research is one of the very few ways of obtaining information in any meaningful sense. The Official Reality, fifty years later, is looked upon universally as a corrupt entity. Ruppelt is interesting because he is half-in, half-out of this sea change in human affairs. Sometimes he trusts his father figures, at other times he does not. We can see in *The Report on Unidentified Flying Objects*, therefore, the first birth of this strange new world where "facts" began to be seen as socio-cultural screens, and input was rarely seen as equalling output. Should it happen to do so, the situation aroused the very worst suspicions that an agenda was forming like a crystal in a jar of salt solution.

In February 1952, just before the birth of Blue Book, Ruppelt received a visit from two officers of the Royal Canadian Air Force concerning the appearance of an orange-red disc that had been seen manoeuvring above a new jet fighter base at North Bay, Ontario, about 250 miles north of Buffalo. These officers, in all likelihood being Intelligence officers, would almost certainly have known about the work of Wilbert Smith[21] and Project Magnet.[22]

Here we see the first sub-cultures of the military industrial complex; we can almost hear project-time fitting itself together. Here is a hive-group full of questing antennae, and bubbling minds and projects for all the world like B-Feature creatures of science fiction themselves. Perhaps this warning from the unconscious is the alien proper. In any case, this was to become the way any and every kind of corporate business was to be conducted in the Western world: here are indeed the seeds and larval forms of the New World Order, all reaching out for their coming host — the high-speed digital computer and the world wide web. At this time, the antennae were merely touching one another in a darkness in which there were a few brief gleams of last light. For example, asking who the "two RAF intelligence officers" were and where their reports are now, would be like asking the Dormouse for the address of the Mad Hatter.

Ruppelt continues, indicating just how hot the whole business was:

A Set of Correspondences

On many occasions Air Force intelligence officers who were stationed in England, France, and Germany, and who returned to the U.S on business, took back stacks of unclassified flying saucer stories.

Did they really? Perhaps the British tax payers should have been told. The plot deepens yet again:

One civilian intelligence agent who frequently travelled between the US and Europe also acted as the unofficial courier for a German group — transporting hot newspaper and magazine articles about UFOs that I'd collected. In return I received the latest information on European sightings — sightings that never were released and that we never received at ATIC through official channels.[23]

The Canadians were seriously interested also. I quote at length because the following passage shows the energy and levels of cooperation that were being established a half century ago. Moreover, these are dynamics which have either vanished, or have become covert. What a change in society has come about since those happy days when an ex-enlisted man could say the following in a popular format. Only Nick Pope has succeeded in doing so in our own time.

For some time, I learned, Canada had been getting her share of UFO reports. One of the latest ones, and the one that prompted the visit by RCAF officers, occurred at North Bay, Ontario, about 250 miles of Buffalo, New York. On two occasions an orange-red disk had been seen from a new jet-fighter base in the area.
The Canadians wanted to know how we operated. I gave them the details of how we were currently operating and how we hoped to operate in the future, as soon as the procedures that were now in the planning stages could be put into operation. We agreed to try and set up channels so that we could exchange information and tie in the project.[24]

But again, in the Escher-Penfold world of the UFO, such cooperation somehow faltered mysteriously with the kind of characteristic vagueness we are discussing: "Our plans for the continuing liaison didn't materialize, but through other RCAF intelligence officers I found out that their plans for an RCAF-sponsored project failed."[25]

"Failure" here appears to be Ruppelt's favourite weasel word for "blocked," and as he continues, he is reduced to giving us winks and nods and hints and glimpses in glorious profusion:

> A quasi-official UFO project was set up soon after this, however, and its objective was to use instruments to detect objects coming into the earth's atmosphere. In 1954 the project was closed down because during the two years of operation they hadn't officially detected any UFOs. My sources of information stressed the word "officially."[26]

Thus does he frequently hint at a shadow world of government and hybrid conspiracies, involving science and technology and the Intelligence community.

THE SHADOW WORLD was present again when on the evening of April 1, 1952, Ruppelt and Colonel Kirkland flew to Los Angeles to attend a meeting of Civilian Saucer Investigators, the first private UFO group created in the United States. This was founded in 1952 by one Ed Sullivan, a technical writer for North American Aviation Corporation. The organisation included scientists from the Los Angeles area, and the most prominent member was Walter Reidel, an ex-Peenemunde rocket engineer and a (supposedly) restructured Nazi, just like Walter Dornberger[27] and Wernher von Braun of NASA. Being the director of rocket engine research for the North American Aviation Corporation, Riedel had some status technologically if not morally.

Ruppelt was distinctly unimpressed by the collection of what he called Don Quixote characters, but he didn't have much time to give more thought to this because he was given an advanced copy of *Life* magazine that contained an article written up from material that journalist Bob Ginna had researched for over a year. The article quoted Riedel, who said he believed that UFOs were from outer space, and his opinion was backed by Maurice Biot,[28] then one of the world's leading aerodynamicists.

Ruppelt didn't have much time to react to all this, because the next morning at dawn found him trying to catch up on some sleep on a United Airlines DC-6, flying back to Dayton to deal with the situation that had been created because of the article in *Life* magazine.

Media Man and the Weasel Words

IN HIS REACTION to the *Life* magazine article, Ruppelt shows that he was getting a better idea of how to deal with media rather than just push it aside as a mildly annoying entity. Though a very straight man psychologically, he now shows that he was more than prepared to play the devious games demanded by the world of personality and image-dominated media. As we know a half century later, facts play a minimal part in media, which is very much a non-cerebral entity. Many a serious and sincere person has gone to a TV studio or has been interviewed for the press, intending to give a prepared lecture only to find themselves ridiculed in the name of entertainment. On television, the sternest rationalists finish up looking like comic action paintings by Salvador Dalí. Even today it takes some people a long time to realise that performance is what is really needed by TV, not facts, which are things as useless to media as they are to a painter or sculptor.

But Ruppelt was lucky. TV as art form (as distinct from knowledge-form) was very young; colour had not yet arrived, and image exploitation was in its infancy. The TV brain had not yet acquired the consciousness to register the handsome young Captain in his glamorous blue Air Force uniform (with medal ribbons) as perfect media fodder for a regular UFO feast. One can only imagine what would happen to such a man today. A present-day Ruppelt would be flanked by lawyers and psychiatrists, accompanied by his mother, his personal counsellor, and constantly on the phone to permanently near-suicidal girl friends. Then would come the scandals, accusations and denials.

Finally, there would come the confession of an abduction experience, later proved "phoney" by "researchers."

Wherever he is now, bless him, Ruppelt will probably thank the gods that he avoided an age in which Truth became Performance Art.

As we look back from such Technicolor possibilities, suddenly time and technology change the pixels of cultural definition, and we have few good images of Ruppelt, who was almost unknown to the general public. It is a pity that, as with George Adamski indeed, Warhol was too young to catch the almost unknown[29] Ruppelt as he caught Marilyn Monroe in his lithographs. If he had caught him, we would see the dropout exposures where Warhol would light up the constituent themes: the wartime bomber navigator, the continuing cerebral growth of a man who had never had a youth, a man born into war machines and given, no less, a final mission into the infinity of the UFO. Behind the handsome head we would see the landscapes of the first great journeys into the inner and outer space of America.

WHEN RUPPELT ARRIVED back at Dayton from Los Angeles, he says, newspapermen were beating down the door. But our hero was now ready to perform. He obviously had learned a trick or two, and was ready for them. The general conclusion about the *Life* article was that no other agency but the Air Force could have sponsored it. Ruppelt's answer was released through the Office of Public Information at the Pentagon. The answer was: "The article is factual, but *Life's* conclusions are their own." Well now, there's our home-time Iowan boy showing he has learned how to move in the ring. He continued:

> In answer to any questions about the article's [sic] being Air Force inspired, my weasel-worded answer was that we had furnished *Life* with some raw data on Specific sightings.[30]

This is a light-hearted expression of course, but nevertheless it shows that our young hero has now become a devious media man despite himself. Reality for him is now becoming inextricably involved with words and style of expression. Image as well as *fact* is become important Performance Art in Ruppelt's head like a B-Feature virus. Gone are his homespun honest truths. Life is becoming complicated; a thing of acts, sets, beliefs and suggestions rather than something purely objective and molecular, as he so assumed it was at his last briefing with General Samford at the Pentagon.

Looking back fifty years later, we can see that here is another sign of the birth of our modern world. As if his appetite has been whetted, Ruppelt gets even more clever at it a few words later:

> My answer was purposely weasel-worded because I knew that the Air Force had unofficially inspired the *Life* article. The "maybe they're interplanetary" with the "maybe" bordering on "they are" was the personal opinion of several high-ranking officers in the Pentagon — so high that their personal opinion was almost policy. I knew the men and I knew that one of them, a general, had passed his opinions on to Bob Ginna.[31]

Human beings are very strange animals. It is truly amazing that the question of the acceptance or rejection of the most tremendous thing that could happen to humanity, namely possible alien contact, is brought down to a matter of which single word to choose. It is an essay in psychology and perception within a very specific background where a very young media is starting to manufacture all kinds of intermediate states between truth and falsehood. Here surely is the very beginning of the blurring of our own virtual world; definite outlines of old mechanical input/output cognition are beginning to become indistinct. Ruppelt can be seen as perhaps one of the last great American innocents, blinking and shaking his head as the certainties of late Victorian fact and fiction begin to blur, and old objective certainty starts to change the goal posts with regard to perceptions of matter and idea, personality and national purpose, technology and information.

He is losing his innocence. He is getting devious. Something else is also happening to him. He is getting bigger and older in his head. His lost youth, strangled by the War, is not dead or gone rotten, but has reared its head in his early middle age. Being still a young man, he is understandably beginning to relish the power he has been given, for perhaps no enlisted captain with such a tiny staff as his ever wielded such power and influence, considering that his mission was somewhat esoteric in military terms. The UFO was relatively young, and so was he. He might not have had the rank, but he was getting the power, status and influence of any General Officer.

The few days after the *Life* article saw Ruppelt absorbed with image and symbolism yet again. Performance Art emerged once more as Project Blue Book was given an official blessing with the issue of Air Force Letter 200-5, Subject: Unidentified Flying Objects. Signed by the Secretary of the Air Force, this order stated that UFOs were to be taken seriously, and it gave Project Blue Book investigators the unprecedented authority to contact directly any US Air Force unit without going through the chain of command proper. Ruppelt swells with pride and not a little astonishment as he says, "This was almost unheard of in the Air Force and gave our project a lot of prestige."[32]

To a certain extent this speeded things up, but again there was the Escher-Penrose version of Catch 22. Since most reports were classified, bureaucracy negated the effect, and Ruppelt had to travel personally to each base and sign a receipt for each report. This was a typical implicit tactic by Air Force authority that runs through Ruppelt's time at Blue Book. There is a trumpet blast, yet they leave him standing at a bus stop fiddling for spare change on his way to a field investigation whose result might change human perception forever, no less. Moreover, a lot of the reports came in the middle of the night, and since Blue Book still had no twenty four hour staffing, Ruppelt was often dragged out of his base living quarters bed or even at home by a phone call from the teletype room at Wright-Patterson. The impression is given that, whilst the Air Force was prepared to make grand paper gestures, it did almost nothing to make those gestures effective, at least through Project Blue Book.

Typical was a report that came in on May 8, 1852. At approximately one o'clock that morning, a Pan American DC-4 (a four-engine prop aircraft) was flying south towards Puerto Rico out of New York City.

It was 6,000 feet over the Atlantic about 600 miles off Jacksonville, Florida. The night was deep black, and after passing into the San Juan Oceanic Control Area, the captain was told that no other aircraft were in the vicinity. This surprised the co-pilot, who was the first to see a light over number four (left) engine, that moved in seconds directly ahead of the DC-4, rapidly increasing in size as it did so, and on a direct collision course. Described as "ten times the size of the landing light of an airplane," the ball of light, accompanied by two other smaller lights, streaked over the left wing, leaving both pilots drenched in sweat.

Exhaustive checks ruled out the usual suspects such as weather, illegal flights (far too fast) and meteors, since no meteors travel straight and level below 18,000 feet. Ruppelt likens this to the Chiles/Whitted incident of 1948,[33] and says he knew "a Colonel" who was convinced that Chiles and Whitted saw a "spaceship."

There was to be an even more memorable interruption of Ruppelt's private life in the same month of May. He had not been home for more than two days per week, when one night he found himself once more phoning Elizabeth, his patient wife, to cancel a babysitter and dinner reservations. On the orders of Colonel Dunn, he was to travel to Washington immediately to see General Samford.

Apparently some of the top people in the CIA had been giving a lawn party to a number of "notable personages," and they had seen a flying saucer. The CIA man described it as a soundless light that stopped for an instant and then began an abrupt vertical climb from the straight and level. As many stared at the light, it finished the climb, levelled off again for a few seconds, then went into a vertical dive to the astonishment of the important guests. Washington filtered out weather, Bolling AFB cleared all balloons and aircraft, and Ruppelt adds that an army chaplain and two teetotaller guests had also seen the light jump!

With reports increasing and Ruppelt hardly able to do the PR job, a civilian, Al Chop, was appointed to the Air Force Press desk. He was a good choice, because he had been through previous publicity battles when he was in the Office of Public Information at Wright Field. Chop was to get his information from Major Dewey Fournet, Blue Book's liaison officer at the Pentagon, with the option of calling Ruppelt if he needed to.

At this time, the Pentagon was becoming extremely interested in the UFO. On average Ruppelt gave a Pentagon briefing once every two weeks to a packed house, and since these meetings were secret, a lot of very hot things were said in this not-on-the-record atmosphere. Ruppelt observed that "in the discussions the words 'interplanetary craft' came up more than once." Matters were such that on May 8 (the same day as the DC-4 incident), Ruppelt, together with Colonel R.J. Taylor of Colonel's Dunn's ATIC staff, was called upon to give an hour-long briefing to the very highest figure in the Air Force, Secretary Finletter and his staff.

By June, Ruppelt considered Project Blue Book organisation was working the way he wanted it to work, given the low scale of resources and staff he had been allotted. At this time his Project Blue Book team consisted of four officers, two airmen, and two civilians on the permanent staff. Major Fournet, the Blue Book liaison officer at the Pentagon, was now working full time on UFO matters, and Ruppelt gives us some idea of the scale of ancillary investigations worldwide, saying that considering the "number of intelligence officers all over the world who were making preliminary investigations and interviewing UFO observers, Project Blue Book was a sizeable effort."[34]

This network had compiled a percentage of unknowns that had, for some time before Blue Book, centred at around forty per cent. This was quite high for a sky supposed to be empty of all and anything but earth-made craft, and his figure was not a simple guess. It was a complex assessment made using many different techniques and technologies, some old, some new, some standard and others quite experimental. However Ruppelt's own personal estimate was that Blue Book "only heard about ten per cent of the UFOs that were seen in the United States."[35]

Let us look at what Project Blue Book base staff did when they were not on aircraft travelling all over the United States checking reports. Given a good report, all available information about weather and research balloons was checked, together with all relevant military and civilian flights. An astronomer (Alan Hynek) was always available for advice, giving up-to-date information on astronomical bodies drawn from journals and almanacs, star charts, and data from observatories. Hydrographic bulletins and Notams (notices to airmen) were often very informative, and every six hours Blue Book received a complete set of weather data from the Air Force Weather Service. Also available for consultation were the Air Force Flight Service, Research and Development Command, Air Defence Command, the Office of Naval Research, the aerology branch of the Bureau of Aeronautics, the Civil Aeronautics Administration, and even the Bureau of Standards on occasion.

Thus did this complete socio-cultural lens strain to get the UFO into focus. It was a complete eye of a particular society, and on occasion it blinked. Knowing people and knowing military and scientific people in particular, Ruppelt gives a era-view of his childhood as he adds, tongue in cheek: "Our entire operational plan was similar to a Model A Ford I had when I was in high-school — just about the time you would get one part working, another part would break down."[36]

The eye needed the high speed digital computer of course, but this was only just beginning its slow development to improve the situation as regards processing and integration of information. As a user-friendly instrument its progress was slow, and by the time it became an almost universal instrument of research and investigation (the 1970s), the Air Force had got rid of the UFO. This was a decision as mysterious as the UFO itself. The question of whether the Air Force was (and is) lying through its teeth is unfortunately beyond the scope of this book, though the question is discussed most effectively in Richard Dolan's *UFOs and the Security State*[37] and Anne Drufell's *Firestorm.*[38]

The exhausted staff of Blue Book worked many hours overtime checking and filing reports from all the various antennae it was hooked up to, but of course only the very best reports could be investigated in the field. Technologically, compared with our own day, Ruppelt had little going for him. He had telephone, telex, and the bulky wire recorder. He had the armed services' fast mail systems and couriers, but he had no modern photocopier, and no electric typewriters. His own good typing ability was a source of wonder at ATIC, where trained secretaries usually did most of the typing work. He had also the booby-trapped Battelle questionnaire and a newspaper clippings service. Certainly compared with fifty years later, as the lens of an investigative eye, none of it amounted to much. But before we smile, it must be borne in mind that, despite our more sophisticated technology, we know little more about the UFO than Ruppelt did.

Entrance to Magonia

HERE IS ONE PARTICULAR incident that shows the kind of sighting Ruppelt had to deal with in summer 1952.

0010 hours on a mainland American fighter base.

Radar registers a 700 mph target slowing rapidly to 100 mph, then showing a slow drift, as if inviting fighters to come out after it. Ruppelt points out that this particular base is not exactly unfamiliar with such incidents. The commanding officer, a full colonel and command pilot, orders two F-86 Sabre jets on the ready line to scramble. But in those early days, few bases had height-finding radar.[39]

The fighters go to their maximum operational altitude of 40,000 feet but can see nothing. The target disappears from the scope as if it were a light being switched off. The ground controller then posts one plane at 20,000 feet and the other at 5,000 feet. The pilot dives down to 5,000 feet, reaching almost the speed of sound. He flattens out, sees a flash below and ahead of him. Then he sees an object. It looks like a weather balloon, but it can't be, because it is moving ahead of him, and he is travelling at nearly 700 mph. He closes to within 1,000 yards, and gets a really good view of the object. The pilot comes within 500 yards of a shape which, in 1952, was beginning to be a familiar object in the skies, according to many reports. Predictably again, the pilot's radio goes dead. Though he tries several times, he cannot contact his buddy flying at 20,000 feet above him, nor ground control.

After a two-minute pursuit (a long pursuit in UFO chase-time) the object starts to pick up speed. The pilot decides to open fire, but as if reacting, the object goes into a steep climb and disappears in a few seconds.

Well, it certainly looks like a good UFO report: a pilot's visual contact after a scramble prompted by a radar response, resulting in the very first offensive shots fired by a military aircraft over the American homeland.

But anyone expecting a vast organization to spring into immediate action with a sympathetic analysis would have been very disappointed.

Any good UFO investigator knows what tends to happen next on such occasions.

It is now two weeks later, and two weeks is a long time in fighter-pilot mental speed.

A phone rings in Ruppelt's ATIC office at Wright-Patterson AFB. It is the Intelligence Officer of the aforesaid fighter base asking Ruppelt to come over, saying he can't talk on the phone. By 1952, Ruppelt knew the signs. It must have been like getting heavy breathing calls. Hardened professionals dare not, could not, or would not speak about UFO incidents for every reason under the sun. Many men with balls of steel nervously requested a very private confessional box whenever there was a question of UFOs.

Again in contrast to his proud claims, Ruppelt cannot get Air Force transport. Just when he is considering looking up the national bus and train routes (what backing this man had!), the Intelligence officer offers to pick him up in a T33 trainer and fly him to the base.

Their parachutes and Mae West lifejackets stowed, the Intelligence officer brings Ruppelt into his office and shuts the door firmly behind him. Ruppelt knows what is to come. The Intelligence officer takes a thick report from the office safe and gives it to him to read.

After what must have been some hours later, Ruppelt is familiar with the story as described above. The Intelligence officer then tells him that he had previously informed the Group Commander that he was going to send the lengthy and detailed report on the incident directly to Blue Book. However, says he, that same commander (whom Ruppelt describes as a known UFO believer, moreover) tells him not to do this without more thought.

One of the reasons Ruppelt was chosen to be head of Project Blue Book was because of his management skills as well as his technical qualifications. But he did less than well in this, his first illustrative instance. He says:

> For some obscure reason there was a "personality clash," the intelligence officer's term, between the pilot and the squadron commander. This was obvious, according to the report I was reading, because the squadron commander immediately began to tear the story apart and accuse the pilot of "cracking up," or of just "shooting his guns for the hell of it and using the wild story as a cover-up."

Cover up? The pilot fired his guns for a lark, and used the UFO story as a cover-up? Fantastic! Following this, the base Intelligence officer and even the flight surgeon, of all people, were all called in to "testify," as if the whole incident had now become a formal trial of the poor pilot's mental and physical abilities. The surgeon, we assume, was brought in because the base did not happen to have handy one of those modern witch doctors called a psychiatrist. The situation became more social-anthropological when Ruppelt adds, "None of them said that he had noticed any symptoms of mental crack-up in the unhappy pilot."

On the contrary, as distinct from what Ruppelt calls the "accused" man, it is the Squadron Commander who exhibits the most extraordinary tribal behaviour, but none are called to vouch for *his* sanity:

> the squadron commander…kept pounding home his idea — that the pilot was "psycho" — and used a few examples of what the report called "minor incidents" to justify his stand.

But according to Ruppelt, the pilot was within his rights to shoot:

> like the authority to scramble, the authority to shoot at anything in the air had been established long ago. Every Air Defence pilot

knows the rules for engagement, the rules tell him when he can shoot the loaded guns that he always carries. If anything in the air over the United States commits any act that is covered by the rules for engagement, the pilot has the authority to open fire.[40]

The Intelligence officer said that during the two weeks since the incident, the Group Commander and he talked over possible reactions to the report. If it went out, they concluded in their wisdom, it would cause a lot of "unnecessary excitement." These are somewhat cautious thoughts for fighter jocks. One imagines what General Curtis LeMay would have said to these serving airmen if had he been in Ruppelt's position. Yet, says the Intelligence officer, both himself and the base commander agreed that if the pilot actually had seen what he claimed, it was vital to get the report into ATIC immediately, to which a tired Ruppelt must have nodded agreement, since as far as the base was concerned he *was* ATIC, standing there before them all in person.

However, continued the Intelligence officer, the group Commander said that he would make his decision after a talk with his Executive Officer, though why he had to take this third opinion is not clear.

From the beginning, then, it is fairly obvious that something has happened to the operational brain of what is, after all, a fighter interceptor squadron on full active service. Ruppelt of course is an Intelligence officer too, but on this day he is not at his best. Any good Intelligence officer would have noticed that the group of men concerned are not acting as they would normally act. Anyone worth their Intelligence salt and who has worked in such or similar related environments knows that third party referrals are only ever used as buck-passing road blocks.[41] On parish-pump committees, fine, but third party opinions rarely have any use or significance in operational fighter squadrons, unless it is for the supply of typing paper or Christmas decorations.

Immediately after the caution about unnecessary excitement, there is revealed something almost as unbelievable as the UFO itself. The Intelligence officer informs Ruppelt that the Base Commander and the said Executive Officer "decided not to send the report and ordered it destroyed." Guess who is going to do the actual burning? The Intelligence officer!

Frankly, such a decision is almost unbelievable. But there are yet more wonders in store. In the face of this recommendation, almost a court martial offense, the Intelligence officer turns to Ruppelt who has just read the report, and asks him what he thinks. The very man supposed to bring the whole situation into focused life comments:

Since the evaluation of the report seemed to hinge upon conflicts between personalities, I didn't know, I could venture no opinion...[42]

He could venture no opinion? What about the radar report, was that a personality, too? Yet in the very next clause (mind you), he offers a definite and rather significant opinion:

...except that the incident made up the most fascinating UFO report I have ever seen.

This must be one of the fastest about-turns in Ufology. To which the Intelligence Officer replied:

I can't give you the report, because Colonel *** told me to destroy it. But I think you should know about it.

There is some amazing cross-logic here. What does "know about it" mean? Does it mean that Ruppelt, the official investigator for the Air Force, was brought along merely to get a tantalising glimpse, and then rely on his memory? What kind of striptease Intelligence officer is this? But Ruppelt, typically, does not get angry and adds, almost nonchalantly: "Later he burned the report."

Amazing! Yet another Air Force vandal acting against his own interests.

So the Intelligence officer flew to Dayton, picked up Ruppelt, only to tell him that the report was going to be destroyed, and he could not have a copy? Most extraordinary!

But unfortunately, this lack of response is sometimes typical of Ruppelt. We have only to imagine what would have happened if, say, Donald Keyhoe had been in Ruppelt's position in this situation. But Ruppelt was no Keyhoe. He manages the situation, he records the information, but he lacks all Keyhoe's manic energy and investigative aggression. Rather like the good scout he always was, Ruppelt comments limply: "The problems involved in this report are typical." Wow, are they really, we ask? Radar returns, dome-shaped objects in the sky, paralysis of the central tactical nervous system of a base designed to prevent a nuclear attack on the United States of America? We might add (almost as an afterthought) probably the most illegal and wilful destruction of raw tactical intelligence. Was that typical, too?

Yes, it appears it was.

OF COURSE RUPPELT intended to write a popular book, but this almost glazed eyed, laid-back attitude of his does not do him justice. He fails to note that a kind of self-induced hypnosis has set in. All actors here have gone quite limp. Each man is performing in quite an extraordinary manner. It should be remembered that this happened to an Air Force unit on active service. The loaded machine guns in the F-86 fighters were not there for training purposes. But as we shall see later during the Washington National Airport sightings, the proper chain of command has collapsed. The unity of the force has been broken, momentarily.

This UFO sighting has done many things. We might just conclude that for a short time the UFO has taken over the unit and has virtually run it. It has caused a crisis, within the management system, of many levels of belief, it has caused an embarrassing personality change, and it has in all likelihood damaged the nerves and trust of the young pilot. It has also caused the most extraordinary behaviour on the part of the Intelligence Officer, the Commander, and the Executive Officer in that they ordered the report destroyed. In other words, momentarily, the Air Force has lost the integrity of part of the nerve centre of an entire unit, and that unit does not know it. The Rendlesham Forest affair was rather similar. A military unit came apart for a short time. It lost its coherence. With their eyes on dramatic things, in this case, no investigator appears to have picked up on the tactical significance of this in military terms.

We can take our pick of the scores of questions that remain. Why didn't Ruppelt complain about the complete waste of his time? Was the Base Commander pleased about the use of a T33 merely to inform Ruppelt that he was not going to get the information he had come for? This flight must have been booked in the base records. What did the Commander think about the Intelligence officer going behind his back to consult Blue Book when he had already ordered the report destroyed without consulting Blue Book? Was Ruppelt at all worried about thunder from above if ever his shrug-shoulders attitude was discovered? No, apparently. Ruppelt did not even cover himself.

Nothing fits here. Nothing at all. The mystery is that Ruppelt is not being devious. He is telling it as it was.

It is curious to note here that not one of the parties involved (including Ruppelt) are serving their own best interests. The Commander certainly would not have lost any points by giving the report to Blue Book. That way, the report would have been cleaned away, and he would not have had much more to do with it. But destroy the report? Well that is utterly fantastic, if not a possible court martial offence; such action may certainly have been against USAF rules and regulations, or indeed an illegal act under Air Force Law.

Actively destroying raw intelligence is an unbelievable folly that might have got all parties concerned either dismissed from the Air Force or placed at least under severe reprimand. The military structure is so hierarchical there is absolutely no element of free will powerful enough to convince someone that raw intelligence should be destroyed on their own singular departmental initiative. This decision and action is just not within the pay-grades of those concerned here. It is strange that the professionals here seem unaware of Rule 1 in any administrative organization. When any organization wants to get rid of something for whatever reason, they never destroy it. That could be professional suicide. No, from the building of the pyramids to the building of the Pentagon, there has been one good standard technique of getting rid of a problem with no trouble at all: you just pass it upstairs, the problem will never ever be heard of again, and you will be praised for your action.

Undoubtedly the report would have been of inestimable value, wherever it landed. It would have given investigators all the radar technicalities and flight characteristics, plus instrument readings, times, speeds, directions, and indeed the dimensions and shape of the UFO. It would surely have been mandatory to preserve a report on at least the malfunction of the aircraft's radio equipment. Meantime, what happened to the national warning net? Surely the scramble was automatically alerted through the grid, if only to pass on any intercept coordinates to another grid reference if the need should arise?

But the group were far away from asking such questions, just as they were far away from asking why there was no sonic bang or ground witnesses.

A complete incompetent mess, in other words. But it is a very curious mess. It is not permanent. It is not like a normal human mess. There is high strangeness at every juncture here. Why did the Commander not take the responsibility of destroying the report himself, if he thought that that was what should happen to it? Did he delegate this action to someone else because he wanted to cover himself? The Intelligence Officer was easily gulled here in this respect. He didn't think fast enough to see that the buck was being passed to him, big time. He allowed himself to become liable for the material act, so to speak, and he didn't even request a written order to cover himself. Certainly most civilians in business and commerce and civil servants would have seen the trick, but this officer did not.

The Intelligence officer was being set up as a fall guy. But he had some options, if limited. He might have taken advice from Ruppelt about his position, or Ruppelt might have suggested taking a look at his legal rights concerning boards, tribunals and indeed civilian litigation if he handed over the report to Blue Book, contrary to orders. Ruppelt might also have offered the Intelligence officer the full backing of ATIC in the event of trouble, but he did not. He did not even advise obtaining a second opinion. The mere mention of the name of Major General Samford might have worked wonders here. That Samford might request the document himself would certainly have prevented its destruction. That General Samford was both the boss of both Ruppelt's ATIC *and* the Intelligence officer also appears to have escaped the notice of all parties concerned.

The best UFO case he had ever received? In that case, surely it would not have been all that difficult for Ruppelt merely to tell all concerned, there and then, that he himself was honour bound to make a formal Blue Book report on this incident, and to add that his request for a copy of the base report was refused by the Intelligence Officer, who stated that he was under orders by the Base Commander to destroy it! Didn't both the Commander and the Intelligence officer think that this was a possibility? Did they really not think that handing in the report to Blue Book would have been the best possible option out of number of options?

In order to try and answer these questions, we have to think right out of the box. We have to face the possibility that for a short time, something very strange happened to this group of highly trained and reasonably intelligent men. Despite their being young, fit men, all fliers, with very good physical responses, every single one of them including Ruppelt himself appear to have gone mentally limp, as if under some kind of temporary hypnosis. As Warriors they are paralysed. They are no longer part of the Air Force machinery of proper command and response. And they didn't even know that they had been attacked.

For a short time, the UFO was running the base, the men and the technology.

The same thing happened at Rendlesham Forest.

SUCH AN HYPNOTIC effect is implicit, and typical of the nature of the UFO experience. There are many examples in Ruppelt's book where even highly motivated and highly intelligent human groups do not behave or think in their usual way both during and after a UFO experience. In this particular case, it is as if a kind of beam came from the UFO itself (B-Feature style again) and for a short time this beam, as it were, reprogrammed the entire spectrum of common information processing within a receptor group. The beam is not electromagnetic. This is the wrong metaphor for something whose technology is more a dimension full of suggestions, whose function is to induce momentary information reprocessing, if only temporarily. If we begin to even think about accepting this kind of idea, then we may have to re-examine all our most fundamental concepts concerning just what a life-form is, and indeed just where life begins and ends, if it ever does begin and end, if indeed the idea of "inanimate" matter is meaningless, and if indeed we may have to accept in turn that in a Web age, information itself may turn out to be an unprecedented form of life.

When we say change, let's think of just what this means in this particular example. Consider what a squadron leader may be required to do on occasion. He has to be God to his squadron. These fliers are not holiday fliers. That means that the squadron leader may, for example, have to talk to a young pilot who has been half-blinded by fragments and blood from a head wound, and is in agony with a thigh shattered by cannon shell fragments. The pilot may be low on fuel and over enemy territory, and his engine giving trouble. Moreover this pilot has to have sufficient confidence and faith in his boss to think that he will cover him and get him back alive. Needless to say, such confidence is not engendered by the behaviour of the squadron leader as here described.

This man has been changed profoundly.

The squadron commander has not so much found a falsehood, or a mistake (he could easily deal with such things with a smile on his face) so much as encountered something that has deeply offended him. For such anger, a vital part of him has been affected. Human beings don't so much reject falsehoods from truth as violently reject that which deeply offends them.

The squadron leader has lost control.

The Commander has become incompetent.

The Intelligence officer is confused.

The fighter pilot is angry and resentful.

And Ruppelt, on this occasion at least, is little more than absolutely bloody useless.

They are all in a kind of momentary sleep. Cultural sleep, that is. The oldest story in the world is of folk waking up and finding themselves covered in cobwebs. This particular sleep didn't last as long as the sleep of Rip Van Winkle, but it was mental sleep nevertheless, a kind of enchantment. Were the B-Feature films right after all, we ask? Were they an unconscious drama trying to tell us something? Yes, there was a kind of forgetting here, an almost-conscious self-erasure of part of personality, role and function. As in sleep, we wilfully give up a piece of the fabric of coherence in order to navigate mentally. Even a partial forgetting is a way of navigation.

Not long after this incident, all concerned will come out of this Escher-Penrose State, and the unit and the personalities will probably function as they always did. For a short time in the canteens and bars they will roar with laughter. At home, they will tell the story for a while to their sons and daughters, as a joke about the day the little green men came to visit the base. They won't tell their families and friends about the scores of unanswered questions. Only when they are alone will they start to remember. Only in private will the secret college of whispers begin about the Escher-Penrose State that they passed through, momentarily.

An Advanced State of Confusion

BY EARLY JUNE, 1952, the Air Force was in what is still described as a "flap" concerning the Flying Saucers. Ruppelt describes a flap in human terms, including a cartoon-joke about ye olde healthy chauvinist sexuality that fortunately is still current:

> A flap is a condition, or situation, or state of being of a group of people characterized by an advanced degree of confusion that has not quite yet reached panic proportions. It can be brought on by any number of things, including the unexpected visit of an inspecting general, a major administrative reorganization, the arrival of a hot piece of intelligence information, or the dramatic entrance of a well-stacked female into an officer's club bar.[43]

For the year of 1948, 149 reports had come into ATIC. In the month of June 1952 alone, ATIC received 149 reports. Summer 1952 was "just one big swirl of UFO reports, hurried trips, midnight telephone calls, and reports to the Pentagon, press interviews and very little sleep."

Ruppelt dates the Big Flap, as he calls it, from June 1, 1952. To get an idea of the pace and the almost impossibility of normal married life, this day was a Sunday, but Ruppelt had been at ATIC all day preparing to fly to Los Alamos the following day to give UFO briefings. Round about five o'clock, the chief of a radar test section for Hughes Aircraft rang Ruppelt to say that new test radar had detected a target at 11,000 feet coming across the San Gabriel Mountains north of Los Angeles. The initial speed was 180 mph, but the target tripled its speed in an impossibly short time for any known aircraft. The target turned, and started to climb right above Los Angeles. The radar plotters were amazed. Whatever it was, according to their calculations, it was climbing at 35,000 feet per minute and travelling at approximately 550 mph. The target then levelled out for a few seconds, went into a high-speed dive and levelled out at 55,000 feet. It then headed out over Riverside, California, and was lost to the radar.

It was an impressive performance, and the Blue Book records held over a hundred cards registering a high-speed climb. However this was the first time radar had tracked a UFO during such a climb. But, given the experience of the crew and technicians, and checking flights, weather patterns and equipment malfunctions, there was nothing Ruppelt could do but register the target as yet another unknown.

In the face of such incidents as this, the mystery of why the Air Force eventually shut down all UFO investigations after the Condon Committee Report in 1969 will be debated for all time, as with the mysteries of the Nazca Lines, the Egyptian pyramids, and the Easter Island statues. Such a complete abandonment ranks with the inexplicable abandonment of cities of the deep past, or certain cultures dying very quickly for no known reason, as pointed out by such terribly abused people as Von Däniken. The denial of the UFO by Authority continues still a half century after Ruppelt. This denial in the face of all evidence and experience is interesting enough in itself, apart from the "reality" of UFOs. The denial has both implicit and explicit elements, plus all the anthropological and cultural interest of the ancient mysteries. The UFO phenomenon, as we shall see, gives an insight also into that modern pyramid culture called the corporate society. In that human beings have a desperate need to disbelieve, we are forced to consider that all cultures navigate by engineered denials.[44]

In this sense, the study of the UFO is not a matter of separating truth from fiction so much as a matter of adjustment. Often we willfully reject embarrassingly obvious evidence in order to give us time to work out a means of absorbing such evidence, and interpreting the changes that acceptance will bring. Thus categories of truth or falsehood are put on hold until we are ready for the experience, whatever that may be. From time to time we lift the curtain again to enhance the working out, then we shut it down again. It is a slow process of steady percolation into our concept-control system. Crude concepts of truth and fiction and rationalizations are nothing in themselves but essential parts of a management system whose function is protective. The truth is that each and every fragment of time and experience is utterly fantastic, quite beyond all possible imagination. Thus skepticism is a control function, and little else. If we are open minded too, soon we could be seriously damaged by what we see and experience. When we lift a stone in the garden, the many different types of creature we see running around are not doing it for fun. They are nearly dead with terror.

The roof of their firmament has been rent in twain.

Mrs. Sohn, Look Out Your Bedroom Window!

DUE TO A MASS of new reports coming at a great rate in the early part of June, just before the Big Flap mounted to a peak, Project Blue Book received yet another higher rating as an Air Force operation. First it had become a project within a group, then a group itself, and now it was a full section, indicative of how important the Air Force regarded the UFO question. The previous Projects Sign and Grudge had never risen any higher than the level of a project within a group. There were the usual human bureaucratic problems, of course. For an enlisted Captain to be in charge of a full group was unheard of; such an organizational rating warranted the rank of at least a full lieutenant colonel. But it was a measure of how Ruppelt was regarded that he was still woefully short as far as adequate communications, equipment, manpower, and resources were concerned.

The Blue Book situation map for early June showed a slight trend of consistent increases on the east coast. Whilst this was on his mind, on Sunday evening, June 15, poor Ruppelt had another one of those phone calls that wrenched him away from an evening with his wife and child. A series of linked reports had come in, and linked reports (the same object seen by a string of different observers in different places) were obviously very important. He checked in at Dayton and read the reports.

The object's slow speed was also very interesting. It travelled only ninety miles in four hours and twenty minutes! Slow speeds such as this, of course, present as many problems as fantastically high speeds. Apart from balloons and helicopters, few airplanes proper can fly below 100+ mph.

He was about to go home when his long-suffering (but very loving and patient) wife called. Associated Press had phoned, she said, and they were hot on the trail of the sighting he was already examining. Ruppelt decided to stay overnight on the base and do some more checking, as if to have some credible story to face the press with the next morning.

After some hours of the usual checks, he was almost convinced that the object had been a balloon. This is just one of many examples of him standing on his head, looking for mundane loopholes.

But equally good reports continued to pour in. On June 18, inexplicable manoeuvring lights were seen for over an hour near Walnut Lake, Michigan, and a UFO paced an Air Force B-25 for thirty minutes in California. On June 19, radar at Goose AFB in Newfoundland registered some very strange targets. Here's Ruppelt gingerly taking off some of the wraps:

> The targets came across the scope, suddenly enlarged, and then became smaller again. One unofficial comment was that the object was flat or disk-shaped, and that the radar target had gotten bigger because the disk had banked in flight to present a greater reflecting surface.[45]

ATIC's official comment was that these returns were due to weather!

Which makes us wonder if they ever said anything else.

Good reports such as these began to mount rapidly at this time. It was not unusual for Blue Book to get as many as eleven "wires" a day. If the letters from the general public were counted, incoming reports mounted to some twenty or thirty per day. Those reports from the general public were, as always, not considered as "good" as the wires from professional folk. Thus a social-group filter was present in even early UFO reports; the implication being (as always) that only the educated intelligentsia and "professionals" are capable of judging what is real or not.

In this sense, reports of landings, contacts, or sightings of occupants within UFOs were rejected automatically by Blue Book, and not even filed. This was knowledge and experience limitation on a grand, institutionalized scale. But all human groups work by means of such psycho-social filters like this, whether their work concerns garden centres, funeral parlours or radar stations and especially courts of law, where truth and fiction can change into one another in a very short time. We limit ourselves to what can be sensibly absorbed otherwise by society, and indeed individuals risk collapse.

Here is a sample of such a rejected report. The utterly fantastic experience about to be described is a mixture of cartoon sketch, schlock fiction and child's toy box. It rejects everything and anything that mature and intelligent people have ever been told, experienced, or expected. As an experience of what we call reality readers of this book will have undoubtedly very great intellectual difficulty in accepting the following experience as valid in any sense whatsoever. But this incident did not occur within the pages of the much abused George Adamski book *Inside the Spaceships*. It occurred outside the windows of a childrens' bedroom in the house of Mrs. Ann Sohn of Prospect Heights, Illinois, sometime in May, 1952, just before the time of Ruppelt's Big Flap. I quote the report made by Captain Runser of CUFOS in full:

Mrs. Ann Sohn put on a pot of coffee and looked at the clock. It was 10:50 PM. She walked into the rear bedroom of her one-storey, ranch-style home to look in on her children, David and Lois, to see if they were covered and to check the window. It was a pleasant evening and the air felt so refreshing that she sat on the foot of her son's bed to gaze out of the window at the stars. The sky was very clear that night.

After about a minute, Mrs Sohn's attention was drawn by a bright light toward the right, and she was amazed to see a brilliantly glowing, round object hovering over the vacant lot next door. The bedroom window faced north and the lot was to the east of her house. There was a screen on the window and Mrs. Sohn pressed her face against it, more closely to observe the object, most of which she was able to see except for the extreme right portion, which was obscured by the corner of her house.

The object, about thirty to forty feet in diameter, was self-luminous and hovered absolutely motionless about 100 feet above the lot for three to five minutes, making no sound. From beneath the object toward the left emerged a cloud of steam or vapour that drifted slowly along the bottom toward the right, giving the UFO an appearance of sitting atop a cloud. Mrs. Sohn was unable to tell where the vapour came from, seeing neither pipes nor any other type of opening. Because the object was above the level of the window, she could determine that the craft was round and not cigar-shaped.

Along the side of the object was a row of about fifteen square windows and just below the windows was a line which Mrs. Sohn described as a seam where the top and bottom portions connected. On the top of the object was a dome which appeared to be made of plastic or Plexiglas. The entire object glowed with a bright white light except for the windows, most of which were dark, and the dome, which had a pale bluish cast similar to the "colour of the blue haze of a distant landscape." Mrs. Sohn's impression was that the dome was illuminated by the reflected light of the rest of the UFO.

Two faint vertical objects similar to poles were visible inside the dome.
Not all of the visible windows were dark; at the far right or rear end were three windows interiorly illuminated by an intense white light. The remaining row of windows were dark, except for some dim blue reflection from the glow of the UFO.

We now brace ourselves for the heart of the matter:

Inside each of the three illuminated windows, Mrs Sohn could see a "crewman." In the first two (moving left to right) the figures seemed to be looking out of the window toward the witness; the third occupant, at the far right, was seen in profile and appeared to be studying a panel of dials or instruments on the wall. As the UFO hovered, the men remained motionless in their positions. Mrs. Sohn tried to awaken her son by nudging him but he remained asleep; her father was asleep in another part of the house, but she was too frightened to yell for him and she was reluctant to leave the window for fear that when they returned, the object would have departed. Her husband was working nights and was not at home.

Next we have pantomime smoke and mirrors, with a touch of Jules Verne's levers:

As Mrs. Sohn was wondering what to do, the figure in the first window (to the left) made a motion with his right hand as if he were pushing forward (toward the window) a lever of some sort. As he did this, a steam of vapour increased; almost at the same moment, he pulled backward on another lever with his left hand, and the colour of the vapour changed from white to green with flecks of orange and then to orange with a few streaks of green visible.[46]

This of course is all very much against our sober work ethic instincts. It sounds like a joke, and it probably is, but not on the part of Mrs. Sohn. That aliens may have evolved from serious linear industrial intention to a form of play (from which all intelligence comes, after all) is deeply insulting to everything in which we believe. It disturbs our profoundly held moral conviction concerning personal and social worth, our cultural input = output equations, and our valued senses both of the serious and the profound. But perhaps our deepest fear is that someone, somewhere, is getting something for nothing. Fifty years ago, of course, there were few if any prophesying that the IQ of the common discursive concentration would drop dramatically, the education system would fail, and that whole parts of Western nations would live completely inside the web-like heads of major media, show business, and rock stars. Even fewer forecast that the Western world at least would become a virtual entertainment panorama, bits of which looked very much indeed like the thing Mrs. Sohn was seeing.

Mrs. Sohn concludes her story:

> Immediately following this, while the figure to the right remained motionless, the figure in the centre window pushed a lever forward with his right hand and the entire ship, except for the darkened windows and the dome, turned a brilliant reddish-orange colour and departed in a shallow climb to the north at an "intense" speed…the three occupants (one of whom never moved at all) were wearing what Mrs. Sohn described as a kind of jumpsuit or coverall with hoods or headpieces that appeared to be part of the suit, covering all of the head except the faces; she therefore saw no hair nor ears on the men…the only other thing she could see besides the figures was the panel of instruments of [sic] dials in front of the man in the window to the right. He appeared to be further from the window than the other two.

A Cross-Examination & More Possible Spaceships

OF COURSE MRS. SOHN's joke from a cornflake packet did not get near to the sober debates of Blue Book. Within just few weeks of this incident, on a day in mid-June, Ruppelt and Colonel Dunn travelled to the Pentagon to give the usual two-week briefing to General Garland, who usually passed on significant information to a very busy General Samford. But this time Samford himself was present, together with members of his staff, and two others that Ruppelt said he was not allowed to name, being certainly Intelligence officials and civilians more likely than not. Prior to this meeting, Major Fournet had told Ruppelt that this extraordinary meeting was in response to the alarming increase in sightings over the past few weeks. This did not refer, of course, to such events as the alarming sighting of the astonished Mrs. Sohn.

Ruppelt started his briefing at 9.15 am in a room in the restricted area of the fourth floor "B" ring of the Pentagon. He discussed the great increase in sighting reports, but insisted in his usual manner that there was still no proof that UFOs were "real," adding that all

UFO reports were merely the misinterpretation of known objects if "we made a few assumptions."

This time, however, he did not get away with what amounted to a bland repetition of what he had said many times previously. Rather did he face for the first time in his life, something of a cross-examination that revealed the vulnerability of his methodology. He was interrupted by an unnamed colonel and, put in the form of a slightly edited dialogue, the result was rather like a Tom & Jerry version of a mediaeval casting out of demons:

> COLONEL: Isn't it true that if you make a few positive assumptions instead of negative assumptions, you can just as easily prove that the UFOs are planetary spaceships? Why, when you have to make an assumption to get an answer to a report, do you always pick the assumption that proves the UFOs don't exist?
>
> [UNEASY SILENCE]
>
> THE COLONEL [continues]: At Goose Bay, the fireball not only buzzed the C-54, it sent the OD and his driver belly-whopping under the command car. Yet Blue Book labelled the report as "Unknown."
>
> RUPPELT: Our philosophy was that the fireball could have been two meteors. One that buzzed the C-54 and another that streaked across the airfield at Goose AFB.
>
> COLONEL: A meteor doesn't come within feet of an aeroplane or make a 90° turn.
>
> RUPPELT: Granted. But these could have been optical illusions of some kind.
>
> COLONEL: What are the chances of having two extremely spectacular meteors in the same area, travelling in the same direction, only five minutes apart?
>
> RUPPELT: I don't know the exact mathematical probability, but it is rather small, I suspect. I have asked our astronomical consultant [Professor Alan Hynek], and he doesn't know.
>
> COLONEL: Well why not assume a point that is more easily proved? Why not assume that the C-54 crew, the OD, his driver, and

the tower operators did know what they were talking about? [...] [With sarcasm] Maybe the ball of fire had made a 90° turn. Maybe it was some kind of an intelligently controlled craft that had streaked northeast across the Gulf of St. Lawrence and Quebec Province at 2,400 mph. Why not just simply believe that most people know what they saw?

To this Ruppelt adds:

The colonel's comments split the group, and a hot exchange of ideas, pros and cons, and insinuations that some people were imitating ostriches to keep from facing the truth followed.

The result of all this was that yet another technological means was proposed to get the UFO into the Cartesian frame of reference. Cameras of long focal length that had diffraction gratings fitted to them were to be placed in UFO hotspots. These gratings acted like prisms: they split received light into spectrum components that could be filmed and analyzed. The proportions and energy elements shown would give a great deal of information about any photographed object, and tell almost certainly whether it was natural or manufactured.[47]

But as Ruppelt says, the UFOs weren't waiting around to be photographed centre stage in the Cartesian frame, or any other frame for that matter; adding, "every day the tempo and confusion was increasing a little more."

By the end of June the east coast in particular was alive with incidents. Jet fighters had been scrambled almost nightly for a week in Massachusetts, New Jersey and Maryland. On three occasions radar-equipped F-94 fighters had intercepted and locked on to solid targets that broke the lock by violent manoeuvres, as if they had themselves registered the radiations from the aircraft.

At 7.25 am on the morning of July 1, a Ground Observer Corps spotter reported that a UFO was travelling southwest across Boston. Neither radar nor F-94s could spot anything, but at 7.30 pm a report came in from a man and his wife at Lynn, Massachusetts, nine miles northeast of Boston. Two vapour trails from climbing aircraft (probably the F-94s) caused them to look up in the sky, where they saw a bright silver "cigar-shaped object about six times as long as it was wide" travelling southwest across Boston, a little faster than the two jets, at an altitude above the vapour trail level. They observed also that an identical UFO was following the first one at some distance behind it. There was also another report made at almost exactly the same time by an Air Force Captain. He was just about ready to leave his home in Bedford, about fifteen miles northwest of Boston and straight west of Lynn, when he saw the two jets mentioned above. He saw also the "silvery cigar-shaped object" travelling south, but did not see the second UFO.

Snowed under by such "good" reports, Ruppelt was helpless; he could do nothing but file the report as "unknown."

We get some idea of the pressure he was under when two hours later, Fort Monmouth New Jersey came back into UFO history. At 9.30 am no less than twelve student radar operators and three instructors were tracking nine jets when two unidentified targets were located. The two targets came in fairly slowly from the northwest, and hovered near Fort Monmouth itself at 50,000 feet for no less than five minutes! The two targets then took off at a speed that was hardly believable, never mind measurable. Whilst the targets were hovering, some radar students went outside the radar room to look at the sky and saw shiny objects at the same time as the radar registration. After plotting these reports, Ruppelt comes as near as he ever does to believing that the objects were intelligently controlled, with all the myriad implications that such recognition would bring:

> Without injecting any imagination or wild assumptions, it looked as if two "somethings" had come down across Boston on a south-westerly heading, crossed Long Island, hovered for a few moments over the secret laboratories at Fort Monmouth; then proceeded toward Washington.[48]

Since the objects were travelling in the Washington direction, reports were expected from that area, and they duly arrived. A physics professor at George Washington University reported a "dull, grey, smoky-coloured" object that hovered for about eight minutes north northwest of the city. During this time, it descended lower and lower until it was so low it was obscured from the professor's view by the buildings in downtown Washington.

The professor added that when he saw the UFO, so did many people in the street, who looked in the air and pointed.

In the face of such incidents, Ruppelt says that the split in opinion so evident in the last Pentagon briefing had closed somewhat, and pro-UFO enthusiasms now gripped the Pentagon, Air Defence Command Headquarters, and even the conservative Research and Development Board.

After a brief lull during which Blue Book received (only!) "two or three good reports per day," on the night of July 12, at least 400 people were cooling off at Montrose Beach in Chicago. It had been a hot day, and many were lying down looking at the stars when they saw a UFO come in from the west northwest, make a 180° turn directly over their heads, and disappear over the horizon. Most people reported a large red light with small white lights on the side. Others claimed that it changed to a single yellow light as it made its turn. It made no sound, and was in sight for about five minutes. Checks on balloons, aircraft and radar revealed nothing. Another unknown. The very next day Dayton itself had a UFO sighting that remained yet another unknown.

By mid-July reports had risen to twenty a day, plus frantic telephone calls from Intelligence officers all over the United States, as every Air Force installation in the US was being swamped with reports. The build up of UFO reports was not limited to the United States. US Air Attaches reported increases in reports from Britain and France, with the South American countries not far behind. Of incoming reports, the forty per cent figure for unknowns still held. Here's the personal scene at Blue Book for mid-July 1952, and we can almost smell the coffee pots boiling over:

> Most of us were putting in fourteen hours per day, six days a week. It wasn't at all uncommon for Lieutenant Andy Flues, Bob Olsson, or Kerry Rothstein, my investigators, to get their sleep on an airliner going out or coming back from an investigation.[49]

Such was the atmosphere, Ruppelt says, that at this time it could be said the Air Force was "braced for an expected invasion by flying saucers." He adds that it could be concluded that one of the beachheads for invasion was, no less, Patrick AFB on the east coast of Florida.

It happened at 10:45 pm on July 18, at the Air Force's Guided Missile Long-Range Proving Ground. Two officers standing in front of base operations noticed an amber-coloured light "quite a bit brighter than a star" at about 45° to the horizon and off to the west. More people came out and looked. It must be realized that the eyes at such a place as this are better eyes than most, and highly trained eyes at that.

In an astonishing display, the light drifted over the base, stopped for a minute, turned, and headed north. Yes, there was a balloon in the air being tracked by radar, but it was nowhere near the light, and there were no aircraft in the district. A second amber light now appeared to the west about 20° lower than where the first one was initially seen and it too was heading north, but at a much greater speed. In another astounding move, the first light stopped and started to move back south over the base.

Whilst the officers and airmen were watching the peculiar movements of the two lights, yet a third light appeared. It came "tearing across the sky, directly overhead, from west to east." Fifteen minutes later, two more amber lights came in from the west, crossed the base, made a 180° turn over the ocean, and came right back over the watching men!

Ruppelt comments:

> They could have been some type of natural phenomenon, if one desires to take the negative approach. Or, if you take the positive approach, they could have been spaceships.[50]

A Dance

UFOs Over Washington

When the Keg Blew

A FEW DAYS PRIOR TO THE SIGHTINGS OF UFOS OVER
Washington in Summer, 1952, a scientist from an agency Ruppelt said
he could not name (either the CIA or the NSA) talked to him for two
hours about the build-up of UFO sightings along on the East Coast. At
the end of this discussion, the scientist ventured a private prediction.
He said that from his study of the UFO reports that he was getting
from Air Force Headquarters and from discussions with his colleagues
(here is Vallee's "secret college" indeed), he had concluded that investigators were sitting on top of "a big keg full of loaded flying saucers."
He continued, punctuating his words by hitting a desk with his fist,
"They're going to blow up and you're going to have the granddaddy
of all UFO sightings. The sighting will occur in Washington or New
York — probably Washington."[1]

The build-up on the East Coast continued as predicted. On July
10, the crew of a National Airlines plane flying south at 2,000 feet
near Quantico, Virginia, just outside Washington, reported a light
"too bright to be a lighted balloon and too slow to be a big meteor."
Three days later another airliner crew flying sixty miles northwest
of Washington at 11,000 feet saw a light below them that came up to
their level and hovered on the left for several minutes, but when the
pilot turned on his landing lights, the object took off in a steep, fast
climb. On July 14, the crew of a Pan American airliner out of New
York bound for Miami reported no less than eight UFOs near Newport
News, Virginia, about 130 miles south of Washington.

At 9 pm two nights later, a high ranking civilian scientist from
the National Advisory Committee for Aeronautics Laboratory at

115

Langley AFB saw two silent amber-coloured lights, "much too large to be aircraft lights," to their right and heading north. This man was a famous aerodynamicist, and Ruppelt adds, "of such a professional stature that if he said the lights weren't airplanes, they weren't."

A man accompanying the scientists also saw these lights, which got abreast of the two men, made a 180° turn and promptly went back to the spot where they had first been seen, appearing to "jockey for position" as they did so. They were joined by yet a third light, and as these three lights climbed out of the area towards the south, several more lights joined the formation!

But all these fantastic events were overshadowed by the events of the very next night when UFOs appeared on radar at Washington National Airport, and there occurred one of the most significant events in the history of the UFO.

They Come: the First Weekend

WASHINGTON NATIONAL AIRPORT, located about three miles south of the centre of the city, at this time had two radars. One was long-range radar in the Air Route Traffic Control Section. This radar, operated by the Civil Aeronautics Administration, had a range of 100 miles and controlled all air traffic approaching Washington. It was known as the Airport Radar Traffic Control, or ARTC, and the senior Air Traffic Controller on duty on the night of Saturday, July 19, 1952, was Harold G. Barnes.

The control tower at the National Airport had radar of much shorter range. This was used to control aircraft in the immediate area of the airport. In addition, Bolling AFB was just east of the National Airport, and in a direct line some ten miles farther east was Andrews AFB, which operated F-94 all-weather interceptors. In turn, both these bases had radars of great power and range, and they were all linked by telephone landlines.

It all sounds like a decent protective screen over America's capital city, but on this night and on following nights, it proved to be anything but that.

According to the logbook of the Civil Airline Association, at Washington National Airport at 11:40 pm on the night of July 19, two radars picked up seven unidentified targets east and south of Andrews AFB. Edward Nugent, an air traffic controller, saw that the targets were fifteen miles away and in a prohibited area. They were just east and a little south of Andrews AFB, and their speed (100 to 130 mph) was too

116

slow for any jet aircraft, and in any case there were no such aircraft in the area. When two of the targets streaked off the screen in an amazing burst of speed, Nugent immediately called in Harry G. Barnes, the senior controller. On seeing the strange display Barnes called Howard Cocklin at the control tower, who said that the tower had seen the targets on the scope, and that at least one of the objects (an orange light) could be seen through the window of the control tower. They reported that strange targets on their scope showed the same slow speed and sudden bursts of speed observed by Barnes, one increase of speed being estimated at 7,000 mph! Of course Barnes' technicians went through their equipment checks, but could find nothing wrong. By this time the targets had moved into every sector of the scope and had flown through the prohibited flying areas over both the White House and the Capitol.

At this point, Barnes decided that the situation in the air over the capital city was sufficiently serious to warrant an immediate fighter scramble from nearby Andrews AFB, but as is the way of mice and men, life is just not that simple. Although Andrews AFB did confirm the targets (Airman William Brady saw an "object which appeared to be like an orange ball of fire"), someone had just forgotten to tell an important person like Barnes that the runways at Andrews AFB were under repair, and the only alternative was Newcastle AFB in Delaware, a hundred miles away.

The commanding officer who did not leave at least one runway in reserve and, say, a two-plane "ready" section for emergencies would certainly have been severely reprimanded in Britain's Royal Air Force. One would have thought that the capital city of the greatest nation in the world at the time of the Cold War would have had good fighter cover. That it had none at all that mattered could have been a court martial offence. It is a mystery to this day that there appeared to be no central, RAF-style, twenty-four hour "fighter command" for the defence, no less, of the whole and entire American government and administration. Unlike standard RAF practice, it appears that there were no twenty-four hour all-weather patrols. For these few significant night hours, the defence of the American nation was in the hands of a single civilian air traffic operator and his few staff who were using standard civilian telephone lines trying (in vain) to choose a suitable base that could launch interceptors over Washington. Thus a man who was not a military man had in his hands what was possibly an immediate War decision.

In other words, in a reminder of both Pearl Harbor and 9/11, the whole and entire chain of US Air Force command, at this moment in time in summer 1952, had collapsed, was hopelessly inefficient, or indeed hardly existed at all in the first place.

Major General J.B. Medaris, retired Army Chief of Ordnance, looking back at this time from 1960,[2] reveals that the contradictory and confused policy of the Air Force was certainly reflective of the general inefficient condition of the high-level staff and planning levels within the US Armed Forces. In a stark reminder of what was to happen later in Vietnam, he comments:

> At the Joint Chiefs' [sic] level, we have probably had the least effective military organization to haunt the United States since the fiascos of the Civil War. It has not only become a debating society, but the unwillingness or inability of the separate Chiefs to resolve their differences has opened the door to usurpation of actual military direction by the civilian elements of the Department of Defence.[3]

Medaris was correct. The situation at the sharp end was just as bad. Astonishing as the UFOs themselves was the state of affairs at Delaware AFB, which did not appear to have a single fighter ready on an RAF-type "scramble" line with pilots sitting in the cockpits ready to lower the hood and scream off the runway. This could be the result of a natural US mindset. In those days the chances of a rapid incoming threat from anywhere but the far north were almost nil, and as we shall see, even the "Russian bomber" threat from this direction was manufactured.[4] Medaris comments:

> The main cause for alarm, according to certain experts, was the great long-range bomber fleet that the Russians were said to be building — a miscalculation that was to cost the American taxpayer untold millions of dollars in fighter planes, fighter bases, and detection devices designed to nullify a threat that never became a full-scale menace. The pressure came from Air Force Intelligence, which had the Russians feverishly building the equivalent of our Strategic Air Command. Actually, they were concentrating on long-range rockets and laughing at us. But they were careful not to laugh too loud, because our calculations suited them just fine.[5]

In other words, the mass of American fighters were way up in the north, and there was hardly anything to spare for the Capital city. The explanation of the delay in dispatching fighters to Washington is therefore most probably once again a reflection, in the tactical area, of the laid-back attitudes Medaris describes. Whatever the reason, not one

F-94 of Eastern Interceptor Command was dispatched for flight when urgently summoned. When a *single* F-94 got to Washington *hours* late, it had little fuel left for playing games with 7,000 mph UFOs!

Early Sunday morning, July 20.

2:00 am, Andrews AFB. Staff Sergeant Charles Davenport reports an "orange-red light" south of the base. At times this light appeared to hover and at other times made abrupt changes in direction and altitude.

2.30 am, Bolling AFB. Staff Sergeant Don Wilson of Bolling's Mobile Control Tower sights a round, red-amber light, which he judged (as an experienced observer) to be travelling at about 1,000 mph.

Meanwhile, back in Harry Barnes' windowless control room, the operators reported that they had a UFO located near Andrews AFB. Lo and behold, the tower staff at Andrews looked out and saw, no less, a "huge fiery-orange sphere" hovering directly over the Andrews Radio Range Station just south of the tower. When normally conservative professional airmen say things like this, we are indeed somewhat obliged to believe them! The three radars concerned (Bolling, Andrews, Washington National) all picked up what we can assume to be was this same target. Such multiple radar/ground observer cross-referencing was a most rare thing as far as UFO sightings were concerned.

Barnes later told newspapers that he thought the UFOs were monitoring their transmissions. This was because by 3:00 am all the targets had disappeared off all scopes just as the *single* F-94 from Newcastle AFB appeared, hours after being summoned by civilian fighter-controller Harry Barnes! This man should have been given a medal for possibly saving his nation, as distinct from a court martial for the commander of the Delaware F-94 squadron concerned.

The F-94 searched the Washington air space but was soon low on fuel and had to return to Delaware. Why could it not land at Bolling (an AFB proper), we might ask, almost vertically beneath the search area, and hence conserve more loiter time? Why could it not land at Washington National itself? Where was the VHF sector net to handle such a situation? Did armed fighters take off on a fully armed operational mission guided by the seat of a pilot's pants, or whatever civilian control he just hoped might be available when he got to the target area? Were the civilian operators at all familiar with military communications, tactics, and rules of engagement as regards interceptions by near-supersonic aircraft?

These are not questions one asks in the military hayseed country described by Medaris, and often by Ruppelt himself. This whole affair was absolutely pathetic. It was a complete shambles. It was, moreover, the result of some deep-laid problems in command and control, in concept and technology that the Air Force had inherited since its birth some six years prior to this event. Medaris was prophetically correct: under the command of General LeMay, the mind of the newly born Air Force was preoccupied totally by the idea of a big-hit nuclear strategic mission, and had little time for anything else other than intercontinental roles. As our example proves, interception over the skies of the central American homeland had not been a high priority, to say the least. Heavy lift, troop transport, communication flights, and airborne early warning for incoming threats suffered likewise. War for LeMay was to consist of one big haymaker punch, not lasting longer than twenty four hours. But as most ring champions could have told him, life is never that simple.

Medaris comments again, with disturbing parallels to 9/11:

> The years have proved that the problems I saw with regard to a separate Air Force were and are far worse than I had imagined. The lack of a sound, experienced, military-technical organization in the Air Force has been responsible for the technical side of that Service becoming almost a slave of the aircraft and associated industries, subject to endless pressure and propaganda. In the area of support to the Army, the situation is also worse than I had envisioned. Operations in Korea very clearly disclosed the inferior capability of the Air Force to provide close tactical air support to the ground Army.[6]

No wonder the Marine Corps insisted on keeping its own air support arm when the Air Force became a separate entity in 1947. When Marines hit the beach, they want air support on call right above their heads, not at the end of a telephone line to someone in the Pentagon, or a squadron of distant heavy bombers whose dismal accuracy presented fifty-fifty dangers to both friend and foe. These considerations may seem somewhat distant from poor Ruppelt's problems, but they were not. They show, in a wider landscape, that they were a part of the frustration that he was experiencing on a smaller scale. We have to consider, therefore, that whilst UFO conspiracies there may indeed have been, such were coupled with an Air Force that on many occasions simply fell apart at the seams, conspiracy or no conspiracy.

We are forced to consider seriously that if the people Medaris describes were given an alien body, they would probably lose it within a very short time.

Hero Hears the News

IN AN INCIDENT which would have made Medaris smile Ruppelt, who was after all heading the USAF's UFO investigation team, only heard about the UFO events of the previous Saturday night/Sunday morning at 10.00 am on the following Monday morning. By lucky chance, he had flown to Washington with the new ATIC Analysis Chief, Colonel Donald L. Bower, for a meeting with Air Weather and Flight Service officials at Andrews AFB. The following day he also had to attend a meeting at the Pentagon to assist in the compilation of an article on UFOs for the *Air Intelligence Digest*. He bought a newspaper in the lobby of the Washington National Airport Terminal Building which was ablaze with news of the UFO visitations.

On reading of the sightings, he phoned Major Dewey Fournet immediately from the airport, but Fournet said in turn that all he knew was what he had read in the newspapers. At about one o'clock Fournet, Ruppelt, and Bower gathered in Fournet's office at the Pentagon and listened to a report from an Intelligence officer from Bolling AFB. This officer told the story of the previous night's events and said he would present ATIC with a full report.

By the afternoon of this same Monday Al Chop, the Pentagon Press Officer, was under siege by the press, some of whom were suggesting that a Congressional Enquiry might concentrate Air Force minds wonderfully. In another room of the Pentagon (the Pentagon always had plenty of rooms ready for the "debating societies" described by Medaris) Intelligence officers were standing on their heads trying to think of what to say to the press. Despite evidence from the incidents, they sure as hell were going to think several times before any announcement that intelligently controlled vehicles not of human manufacture had invaded the night skies of Washington.

This whole scene here is an essay in complex cultural denial. To be fair to the Pentagon PR staff, it was no small problem that they had been landed with. The situation was not about a possible new Russian aircraft, a new spy revelation or a contractual fraud. No, this was an inch away from admitting an alien invasion, of all things, and this was only the start of the Intelligence week! Well, in the face of that, it is no wonder that men used to dealing with somewhat mundane matters found great difficulties in coping with a situation straight out of a B-Feature film. Men used to super-clerking and the blandness of PR statements, men used to manufacturing wholly complimentary brochure-style publicity (with Betty Grable on the front in a swimsuit) about the wonderful Air Force, were faced with taking a step downstairs and announcing (if the straw poll went their way) the very mother of all invasions.

Who was going to do that? Never had a set of staff minds had such a predicament hoist upon them. The effect was like trying to put a cluster of jet engines on a set of roller blades. Men with the minds of accountants and administrators and solicitors were being asked to mutate virtually, go through a thousand years of change in their heads, or indeed choose some lesser minion to go out and announce that the Coming was hereby come. This would give the said minion an immortality he had not perhaps expected after kissing honey and the kids goodbye that morning and motoring to the Pentagon to check on the stock of woolly socks for base guard patrols. When immortality is near it needs strong and great men to grasp the wreath offered, and there were simply no great or strong men around in the United States Air Force, up to the task at this time.

Yes, by this time the Pentagon was a corporation and corporation men do not rock boats. An announcement was at least worthy of a rebel, and the Pentagon was the last place in the world to find one. Gone were the days of faces and names of men who might have handled the situation, warriors such as Billy Mitchell, MacArthur, Pershing, or Patton, or indeed the semi-disgraced Lindbergh, the one man who might indeed have had the bottle to go out and announce that the aliens were here. But no, the New Man was Bland Man, and the Bland Man is Nobody, and Nobody is invisible. Thus the Pentagon refused to grasp the wreath that was offered.

This is how bureaucracy works. Here is how, as a systems-animal, the corporation hides things. Sometimes there is blood and conspiracy, but here is shown a far more effective technique: just a natural scaling down until an individual's power levels are almost zero, and he can do nothing but go through the motions of compromise and failure.

This is how the corporation works. From the 1950s onwards, many hundreds of very different B-Feature films have pointed towards the cellular structure of the corporation itself as the alien's hive, or nest.

What now followed was pure Kafka. This author gives no apology for quoting in full, for here is Ruppelt seeing himself almost as a character in a novel, a loner in the metaphysical city. Given the events in the night sky when darkness falls, the city is a Washington consisting of fractured and splintered planes like a picture by Escher. In vain does Ruppelt try to make this Escher city Cartesian again, put the right-angles and the logic back again into the Washington he knew, like a good husband after a burglary or a burst boiler.

But he cannot get the furniture back in place.

The same day, 4:00 pm.

Under siege from the press, and with no help from the Air Force, our hero is left trying to bat every ball America can throw at him. He stalls the press with a "no comment," perhaps knowing that this will only make matters worse. He calls Lieutenant Andy Flues, whom he has left in charge back at Dayton. He tells Flues that he has decided to stay over to "investigate" the Washington sightings. Andy Flues does not improve his mood by informing him that they were all in a "deluxe flap" back at Blue Book HQ. Reports were pouring out of the teletype machines at the rate of thirty a day, and Ruppelt comments, "Many were as good, if not better, than the Washington incident."

Here is how the official "investigation" of the United States Air Force into the first wave of Washington UFO sightings proceeded:

Feeling like a national martyr because I planned to work all night if necessary, I laid the course of my investigation. I would go to Washington National Airport, Andrews AFB, airlines offices, the weather bureau, and half a dozen other places scattered all over the capital city. I called the transportation section at the Pentagon to get a staff car but it took me only seconds to find out that the regulations said no staff cars except for senior colonels or generals. Colonel Bower tried — same thing. General Samford and General Garland were gone [with a possible alien invasion pending, they would be — author], so I couldn't get them to try to pressure a staff car out of the hillbilly who was dispatching vehicles. I went down to the finance office — could I rent a car and charge it as travel expense? No — city buses are available. But I didn't know the bus system and it would take me hours to get to all the places I had to visit, I pleaded. You can take a cab if you want to pay for it out of your per diem was the answer. Nine dollars a day per diem and I should pay for a hotel room, meals, and taxi fares all over the District of Colombia. Besides, the lady in finance told me, my travel order to Washington covered only a visit to the Pentagon. In addition, she said, I was supposed to be on my way back to Dayton right now, and if I didn't go through all the red tape of getting the orders amended I couldn't collect any diem and technically I'd be AWOL. I couldn't talk to the finance officer, the lady informed me, because he always left at 4.30 to avoid the traffic and it was now exactly five o'clock and she was quitting.

If only to avoid arrest through being AWOL, our hero decides that he too is quitting, and for once we don't blame him:

At five-one I decided that if saucers were buzzing Pennsylvania Avenue in formation, I couldn't care less. I called Colonel Bower, explained my troubles, and said that I was through. He concurred, and I caught the next airliner back to Dayton.

I leave readers of this book to imagine the edifying spectacle of Ruppelt behind bars as the aliens declare themselves, and stalk on webbed feet towards the White House.

Interlude Between Invasions

BACK AT DAYTON, still a sucker for Cartesian punishment, our hero reaches the bottom of the curve of human responses, once more in the form of Captain "it's all weather" Roy James of the radar branch of ATIC. Captain James, a character straight out of Kafka, of course knows nothing whatsoever about the Washington experiences, cares even less, and says that he thinks the radar targets were due to weather, adding, "but since he didn't have the finer details he naturally couldn't make any definite evaluation."

What wonderful candidates for leadership and initiative courses all these people are! Here is a passage, written in the early 1950s, from William H. Whyte's classic book, *The Organization Man:*[7]

> Among Americans there is today a widespread conviction that science has evolved to a point where the lone man engaged in fundamental research is anachronistic, if not fundamental enquiry itself. Look we are told, how the atom bomb was brought into being by the teamwork of huge corporations of scientists and technicians. We don't really need any more ivory-tower theorizing; what we need is more funds, more laboratory facilities, more organization.

The corporation as a collective works its way towards its secret agendas by atrophying deviant energies through physical and mental exhaustion. It is a better way than murder because the victim still appears to be alive. But as a teacher at any level will tell, sustained contact with poor minds is as exhausting as a physical journey. They absorb energy without giving anything in return, and they are hardly built for intellectual adventure. There are signs towards the end of *The Report on Unidentified Flying Objects* that Ruppelt is getting tired of being surrounded by some of the most abysmal corporate mediocrities that a man could possibly meet.

In other words, he is being steadily drained not only of resources but also of imagination and energy. If paranoids like to think this was the result of an agenda, then they have good reason to come to such a conclusion.

After facing Captain James, Ruppelt has the slightly less grim task of trying to deal with sightings that have now reached the level of forty a day, with about a third of them classified as unknowns.

On July 18, more amber lights had been seen at Patrick AFB, Florida. In Uvalde, Texas, a UFO described as "a large, round, silver object that spun on its vertical axis" was seen to cross a wide arc of afternoon sky in forty eight seconds. At Los Alamos (a restricted area for flying), and at Holyoke, Massachusetts, UFOs had been chased by jets and in two night encounters, one in New Jersey and another in Massachusetts again, F-94s tried unsuccessfully to intercept unidentified lights reported by the Ground Observer Corps.

On July 23, Jack C. West, Commanding Officer of the 142nd Fighter Interceptor Squadron based at Newcastle, Delaware, said his jets were ready to go into action "at a moment's notice."

In the midst of such promises, our exhausted (but distinctly unimpressed) hero shuffles paperwork, and says, as if to reassure readers that he is still alive, more than anything else:

> Copies of these and other reports were going to the Pentagon, and I was constantly on the phone or having teleconferences with Major Fournet.[8]

This is a plaintive, rather mournful note, tinged with a little growing bitterness. Our hero is going through the motions expected of him, but the corporation is rubbing him out. He is also becoming a mite suspicious that there are many other mysterious hunters in the woods more powerful than he.

In his rediscovered second youth, he is passing from innocence to experience very quickly. As we shall now see, our hero is still clinging to hopes that are going to be dashed as sure as were Jack West's optimistic estimate of his squadron's reaction time.

Our man is getting a little tired.

Months ago, he might have suggested to the Pentagon that a trundling old C-47 with wide-cut windows for cameras and other equipment would have been far better than an expensive interception by an F-94. With additional gas tanks for low speed loitering, a C-47 could have stayed up for the better part of a day or night and produced much more information from a mass of varied instrumentation. After all, air combat was not the primary object here.

But at this late stage in his Blue Book career, Ruppelt now knows better than to suggest such brilliant, cheap, and effective ideas to the straight conventional minds at the Pentagon.

Perhaps also by this stage he has learned something even more important. Perhaps in some inner recess of his once innocent mind he now knows that an old C-47, though far more effective, would not *look* nearly as good as a useless F-94.

Perhaps also he is now learning that style is what corporations are all about.

They Return: the Second Weekend

RUPPELT FIRST HEARD about the second wave of Washington National sightings exactly one week after the first wave. On Saturday, July 26, Bob Ginna of *Life* magazine phoned Ruppelt to ask what the Air Force was doing about the matter of UFO sightings in the Washington night sky, some of which were being made almost as he spoke. With no little bitterness, and obviously with the sad taste of his last visit to Washington the previous week, our hero replied, "I have no idea what the Air Force is doing; in all probability it's doing nothing."[9]

After Ginna's call, Ruppelt then called the Intelligence Duty officer in the Pentagon. He had been correct in his prophecy about the Air Force. They had not even heard about the sightings (taking place almost directly above their heads, moreover!) never mind considering doing anything about them. Ruppelt, miles away in Dayton and with memories of his financial and administrative difficulties the week previous, did not exactly rush to the Washington scene. He asked the duty officer to get in touch with Major Fournet and ask him to go to the airport, which was only two or three miles away from Fournet's home in Washington. After getting the call, Fournet picked up Lieutenant Holcomb, a Navy electronics specialist assigned to the Air Force Directorate of Intelligence. Holcomb was obviously a good man to have around in this situation, and the pair drove to the radar room at the National Airport, finding the quick-thinking and astute Al Chop already present. As Ruppelt comments, at least this time there was some kind of control group monitoring the situation as it developed. But we note again that this was the result of a small scale, low rank improvisation by four men, of whom one was a civilian, and another stranded some 380 miles away.

What a command and control system this was!

Up to this moment in time, there was absolutely no sign of the interest or presence of any kind of functioning mind within top Air Force echelons. At no stage in this week-long saga were the Chiefs of Staff involved, informed, briefed or alerted concerning the presence of intelligently controlled, unidentified flying objects maneuvering over the capital city of their nation.

Given the worst possible scenario, the entire nation could have been wiped out whilst Chiefs of the American Armed Forces prepared to go to their beds. In vain we ask the question, where was any operational dimension of the wretched Air Force? Perhaps someone should have told them that during the weekend prior to this second incident Harry Barnes, a civilian, was ordering fully armed fighters all over the Washington night sky as if he were the Air Force Commander in Chief. That such decisions should have been his alone is as utterly fantastic as the UFOs themselves, demonstrating that rational fantasies are just as fantastic as any other type.

Obviously, the sleeping Air Force HQ was not going to help this group put together in a hurry by Ruppelt; HQ did not even know about this group, they did not even know of the situation in the very air above their heads! It is a classic case of a major HQ being utterly out of touch with a rapidly developing situation, and should be made a case study in military staff colleges. It won't be made such of course, because fifty years later it is still extremely embarrassing.

Of course on a minute scale, from the point of view of military command psychology, this state of mind of General Vandenberg's Air Force HQ parallels the French collapse in 1940, and Haig's tactics during the Somme battle in 1916. Here is a similar classic case of tactical paralysis, easily equivalent to the failure of the tanks of the Guards Armoured Division to reach 1st Airborne besieged in Arnhem in 1944. It would have been God Help America if on this night the Russians had decided to make a serious move, or if the strange lights had indeed been theirs which fortunately, as we now know, they were not.

Meanwhile, back at Dayton, our hero was pacing the floor knowing not quite what to do. Perhaps to amuse himself, he phoned the same Captain Roy ("it's all about weather") James mentioned several times in this book, and he comments, tongue in cheek:

> I did call Captain Roy James thinking possibly he might want to talk on the phone to the people who were watching the UFOs on the radarscopes. But Captain James has a powerful dislike for UFOs — especially on a Saturday night.[10]

Here we are faced with, I contend, the onset of that American corporate military decadence that led to Vietnam. The poor minds, the poor concentration, the crass amateurism and atrophied mental sinew are the same. No wonder all space projects were taken from the US armed forces and given to infinitely brighter civilian scientists, technologists and engineers under NASA. Given the kind of poor mind Ruppelt was meeting in the mid-grade level of the US Air Force, space projects would have been intellectually quite beyond the mental level of that organization, bless its brave heart.

But back now to our hero, still pacing his room at the Air Technical Intelligence Centre at Wright Patterson Air Force Base, expecting a phone call from Washington about a possible alien invasion, no less. At five o'clock on the following Sunday morning, Ruppelt got his call from Major Fournet who gave him the story of the events of the previous few hours. It was a hell of a phone call and a hell of a story. It went something like this.

At 10.30 pm on July 26, with reporters and press photographers crowding into the radar room with the Fournet group, the very same radar operators at the National Airport who had seen the UFOs the week before, now started to pick up the same slow-moving targets on their flat, twenty-four inch screens. This time the UFOs were spread out in an arc around Washington from Herndon, Virginia, to Andrews AFB. Again, both the control tower and Andrews AFB registered the same targets.

By 11.30 pm four or five targets were still being continually tracked, and a call was made this time to Newcastle County AFB for Jack West's "instant reaction" interceptors. Poor Jack must have been considerably embarrassed, for once again there was some delay. But when two F-94Cs did arrive, all targets promptly disappeared from the scopes, as if confirming senior controller Harry Barnes' prediction from the previous week that "they" were listening to the VHF.

The F-94C pilots saw nothing, even though there was excellent visibility. Having at a maximum only twenty minutes' loiter time over the area, the fighters had to leave but as soon as they did so, the UFOs came back on the scopes!

What neither Fournet nor Ruppelt could know at this time was that a few minutes after the targets disappeared, people in the area around Langley AFB near Newport News, Virginia, started to call Langley Tower to report that they were seeing bright lights that were "rotating and giving off alternating colours." The Tower operators themselves, on seeing a similar object, called for an interceptor. An F-94C was vectored towards the approximate position of the strange light, but as soon as it got near, the light went out "like somebody turning off a light bulb." Nevertheless, the F-94C got three radar lock-ons, only to have them broken by this now invisible, "solid" object.

True to form, as soon as the F-94C left the Newport News area, the targets came back onto the scopes at Washington National.

With the targets back on the scopes, the controller decided he had had enough of calling individual air bases, with their scandalous response time, and called the Air Defence Command directly. This appeared to concentrate minds wonderfully, and almost immediately two F-94Cs roared south towards Washington (from Delaware AFB) just after midnight. In an almost unprecedented move, all civilian traffic was cleared from the area. As if the UFOs wanted to confuse by exhibiting any and every kind of behaviour, this time the targets stayed on the scopes when the fighters arrived.

As the lights and the fighters closed, this was a very tense moment indeed in modern American history, although no conventional historian mentions it. All present in the Tower and in the other locations thought they were going to witness the first contact of an aircraft with a UFO, though what was going to happen to the pilots of the F-94C (or indeed themselves), no one knew.

The two F-94C pilots were Captain John McHugo and Korean veteran Lieutenant William Patterson. The former, though vectored towards strong radar returns, saw nothing. The latter, vectored to a target ten miles outside Washington, saw four white "glows" and closed in for the expected intercept. Researchers Connors and Hall report that Al Chop later told them of a truly haunting moment when

> the orb-like lights came right at Patterson and clustered around his aircraft. Desperate for a course of action, Patterson radioed ARTC (Airport Radar Traffic Control) for assistance. He simply did not know what to do. [11]

That Patterson was on an armed operational mission over Washington (a mission with possible war potential, moreover) and had desperately to ask civilian controllers for (combat!) permission, shows the absolutely amazing state of decay within the air interception system of the United States Air Force. We ask, our hair standing on end, where was Patterson's Eastern Area Defence Controller? We might as well ask where were the Chiefs of Staff, or indeed the President himself.

Al Chop went on to tell Hall and Connors:

> There was stunned silence among the tower personnel at that mo-

ment. No one could say a word. Patterson was on his own. Fortunately, the orbs then pulled away from Patterson's aircraft.

The press was fortunate enough to get the first pilot interviews almost as soon as the returning F-94Cs of McHugo and Patterson were back on the runway. The presses rolled, and quoted Patterson as saying:

> I tried to make contact with the bogies below 1,000 feet, but they [the radar controllers] vectored us around. I saw several bright lights. I was at my maximum speed, but even then I had no closing speed. I ceased chasing them because I saw no chance of overtaking them. I was vectored into new objects. Later I chased a single bright light which I estimated to be about ten miles away. I lost visual contact with it at two miles.[12]

Meanwhile, back at Dayton other reports continued to come into ATIC on an almost hourly basis:

> We kept them quiet because we weren't able to investigate them right away, or even confirm the facts. And we wanted to confirm the facts because some of the reports, even though they were from military sources, were difficult to believe.[13]

You can say that again, Edward Ruppelt!

Selling Rationale: The Samford Press Conference

THE FOLLOWING MONDAY morning of July 28, Ruppelt left yet again for Washington in the company of Major Ed Gregory, another Intelligence officer at ATIC. Once again, on arrival Ruppelt bought a newspaper with banner headlines about the incidents of the previous Saturday night and Sunday morning. In the face of all lack of leadership and high command liaison, this is how two Intelligence officers of Project Blue Book received information in July, 1952. It reads like a Hank Jansen popular novel of the time:

> On our way through the terminal building to get a cab downtown, I picked up the evening papers. Every headline was about the UFOs:
>
> FIERY OBJECTS OUTRUN JETS OVER CAPITAL — INVESTIGA-

A Dance

TION VEILED IN SECRECY FOLLOWING VAIN CHASE

JETS ALERTED FOR SAUCERS — INTERCEPTORS CHASE
LIGHTS IN D.C. SKIES

EXPERT HERE TO PUSH STUDY AS OBJECTS IN SKIES REPORT-
ED AGAIN.

Ruppelt was amused to find that he was himself the "expert"
concerned, and when Major Gregory and he walked into the lobby of
the Roger Smith Hotel to check in, reporters and photographers "rose
from the easy chairs and divans like a covey of quail." But Ruppelt was
an old hand at this game by now, and managed to reach the elevator
without even a "No comment" and refused to pose for pictures. This
made things worse, of course, and in Ruppelt's own words, there
resulted a "junior-sized riot."

The next day was a day of equal confusion. Again, we have a
model for complete tactical shock within a military organization. In
the staff colleges of many major countries, there is a joke-prize given
to the candidate who provides most excuses for not keeping on the
move, getting information, and attacking. US Air Force Intelligence
could have won this booby prize in 1952. Ruppelt comments on the
confusion, adding:

> There was a maximum of talk and a minimum of action. Everyone
> agreed that both (Washington) sightings should be thoroughly
> investigated. But nobody did anything.

Like headless chickens, Major Fournet and Ruppelt spent the
entire morning "just leaving" for somewhere to investigate "something." Every time they would start to leave "something more pressing
would come up."

In this atmosphere something just had to give, and give it did.
At 10:00 am Ruppelt received a telephone call from no less a person
than Brigadier General Landry,[14] the President's Air Aide. Landry
had phoned at the personal request of President Truman, no less, to
try and find out just what had been going on in the very air above his
sleeping head during the previous Saturday night and Sunday morning.
Again, the tribal scaling is interesting: the President of the United
States is just one move away from getting in almost direct touch with
a lowly Air Force Captain to get information about something which
could be possible nuclear annihilation, or on the other hand, possibly

the greatest thing that ever happened to mankind!

Many people who should know better still ask why a quiet little man like Truman ever got to be President. His action on this occasion tells them why. Truman went straight to the organ grinder and not the monkey. We note that neither he nor Landry telephoned the General Staff of the United States Air Force.

We also note that the quiet little man was listening to the phone conversation.

Truman, probably as a result of a report by Landry after the phone call, took immediate action. The historian Professor Michael Swords reports that on this same date Truman, in a meeting of the National Security Council, asked the CIA to look into the whole UFO matter. General Walter Bedell Smith ordered the Agency to get to work on this matter immediately. The result was that Fred Durant, a CIA specialist in chemicals and rocketry, got in touch with Major Dewey Fournet almost immediately, and thus opened the very first UFO channel proper to the CIA, about which Ruppelt probably knew nothing. Swords quotes Fournet as saying:

> I knew he [Durant] had been given the authority to see me and I was told that I could tell him everything that I possibly could about the UFO Project, from Day One. I did know he was on the CIA payroll. I assumed he was just one of the project managers, and, there again, you don't go asking questions like that of those people.[15]

This is a typical expression of the fear generated by those secret Intelligence agencies that were to become so influential a part of the military industrial structure. It is not well known that the original Men in Black were created by Kafka. As modern demon-figures, the MIBs worked their mythological way through both Communism and Nazism before they reached the UFO culture and the military industrial complex almost at one and the same time.

Round about mid morning on the following day, Tuesday, July 29, Major General Samford, Head of Air Force Intelligence, announced that a press conference about the weekend sightings would be held at 4:00 pm that afternoon at the Pentagon. That it was the largest and longest press conference the Air Force had held since its formation in 1947, is a measure of its importance.

The meeting was organised by the Department of Defence in Room 3E-869 of the Pentagon. Accompanying Major General Samford on the dais were Major General Roger Ramey,[16] Director of Operations, USAF; Colonel Donald Bower and Captain Roy "Weather" James of the

Technical Analysis and Electronics Branch of ATIC, and Mr Burgoyne L. Griffing, a civilian attached to the Electronics Branch of ATIC. Ruppelt was on the platform, but he was out-ranked by two Generals and a full Colonel and, apart from a few remarks, our hero did not shine on this occasion, but then neither did anyone else present. It was an ominous sign that whilst Roy James was on the platform, Al Chop, Fournet and Holcomb were not. That hot reports from front line soldiers who had been on the scene were not required was another ominous sign. Yet the Press at the time described General Ramey as "being in charge of jet interceptions over Washington at the time of the UFO flap," and after the press conference, both Samford and Ramey were referred to as "the Air Force's top two saucer experts."

So much for poor Captain Ruppelt!

Samford's own performance was anything but impressive. Frankly, he was out of his depth. He was a distinguished staff officer[17] who had served well in administrative positions, but he was hardly at home in what was after all the hot seat of an operational command appointment. He was quite opposite in character and disposition to the dynamic and thrusting General Cabell, who had held the post before him. As such he lacked all personality and field-leadership qualities. He hated even healthy controversy, confrontations, personality clashes, and like a typical nineteenth century savant, those things called *enthusiasms*. He struggled for verbal expression, and produced a weird and wonderful variety of responses, some puerile, some quite mistaken, all peppered with his own special style of nervous blandness typical of a staff administrator most uncomfortable before the press and public. He was not properly briefed, his concentration faltered, and his knowledge of basic science and technology was poor. In this respect, Samford's appointment in 1956 as head of the National Security Administration was very strange, considering that he did not have anything like the great synthesising brain required (presumably!) for such a post. He was in all certainty one of those members of an establishment who serve as figureheads more than anything else, and he had only a four year run at NSA before he retired, which rather speaks for itself.

Keyhoe, writing in *Flying Saucers from Outer Space*, is of the opinion that Samford didn't want to hold a press conference about the Washington sightings; not only did he not consider himself the man for such a thing, he knew that certainly many of the questions he would be faced with would contain complex imponderables that no man on Earth could answer or resolve.

However, a press conference had to be called, and under pressure from General Twining[18] the Chief of Staff, the reluctant Samford was forced to grasp the nettle. If this was a cover-up (as was most likely), then it was ill prepared, amateur and unimpressive, exhibiting top-of-the-head contradictions and ambiguities at every turn. The only really sinister element in the whole resulting circus was the presence of General Ramey, the man accused by many authors of covering up the Roswell evidence.

As if the saucers were aware of this meeting, that very morning they had put on a good show. Army officers and Indiana State Police had watched a strange "dogfight" between several discs over Indianapolis. Three hours later a UFO was detected within the restricted air space over the Los Alamos laboratory complex, only to disappear when chased by jets. The previous night the Independent News Service had reported the issuing of a new Air Force order saying that if UFOs refused to obey orders to "land" (presumably issued by local or airborne VHF) pilots were to open fire. Frank Edwards, another popular author of Keyhoe's ilk, put the details of this on the Mutual Radio Network. A flood of protests about the Air Force statement came in from many listeners, most of whom reacted as if the order entailed some obscene animal cruelty. There was thus great psychological empathy for the UFO, which brought forth sympathies as if for some mighty magical beast of legend. That it so obviously baffled and annoyed all constituted authority was also good for public sympathy.

Robert L. Farnsworth, president of the US Rocket Society, personally wired the White House and gave United Press a copy of the wire. It read:

> I respectfully suggest that no offensive action be taken against the objects…should they be extraterrestrial, such action might result in the gravest consequences, as well as alienating us from beings of far superior powers. Friendly contact should be sought as long as possible.[19]

By 3.30 pm the conference room was already half full. Present were C.B. Allen, aviation correspondent for the *New York Herald Tribune*, Gunnar Back, television presenter, Clay Blair from *Life* magazine, and Doug Larson of North Eastern Airlines. Also present to witness this important (and often hilarious) moment in Western techno-military time was Donald Keyhoe himself, whose brilliantly critical books had been a regular thorn in the side of the Air Force for some years. An ex-aide to Lindbergh and an ex-Marine pilot, Keyhoe was a brilliant and relentless man. His one task was to try and force an admission from the Air Force that UFOs were solid objects exhibiting intelligent behaviour. His manic energies and his good critical intelligence alone were in direct contrast to the senior military men before him on the platform, who were rather like a collection of miracle debating Cardinals of the deep past. At times, indeed, during this meeting, one can almost hear the firewood being piled under the martyrs' feet.

Samford himself was a man far too well adjusted to be of the highest intelligence. He had certainly a high level of commonsense and practicality, but secured promotion through long administrative service more than anything else. Like Albert Speer, the Nazi Armaments Minister, Samford was a high-level *apparatchik* commissar, although doubtless of infinitely greater moral worth. Such superb techno-bureaucrats can usually successfully vanish anything and everything, from millions of corpses or in this case, UFO sightings. Like Speer again, Samford, in typical corporation style, managed from behind as distinct from leading from the front.

All the actors here on display were pre-television entities, but yet again like Speer, Samford would have been perfect for the bland medium. He was the perfect smoothie, made for the sound bite and the sentence that, as we shall see, gives no information at all. With his good-natured, patient condescension he would have been perfect also for that piece of instant throwaway consumable of our time called the "factual" documentary, then in its gloriously innocent black and white infancy.

The press conference[20] was about business management of information and concept, style and administrative power. It had nothing to do with truth, the Air Force, or the UFO. Samford again might almost have been the smooth Albert Speer describing some monstrous project and just forgetting to mention (as Speer did) the millions of corpses under the foundations. This was what Samford was really good at: the perfect management of the perfect expression of the perfect Cartesian moment of an act of vanishing equivalent in Samford's case to intellectual murder as distinct from physical.

The corpses here are not those produced by forced labour, but are those mortally wounded by the smothering of the impossible speeds and accelerations, the equally impossible manoeuvres, the quasi-materiality, the radar/witness triangulations, and gun-camera images involved in the UFO phenomenon. Here are Charles Fort's "damned" events, and here is the full rehearsal for the Condon tribal *fest* to come thirty years later.

Talking of the high percentage of unknowns, Samford says:

However, I'd like to say that the difficulty of disposing of these is largely based upon the lack of any standard measurement or any ability to measure these things which have been reported briefly by some, more elaborately by others, but with no measuring devices that can convert the thing or idea or the phenomenon into something that becomes manageable as material for the kind of analysis that we know.

Thus is the Cartesian frame a boundary exclusion paradigm. That which cannot be measured is not *real*. Therefore, only godless mechanism is real. Goodness only knows what we do with the things that cannot be measured, such as goodness, love, mercy, charity, music, poetry, mystical experience, and many other non-measurable things such as spiritual or holistic elements that alone make life meaningful and worthwhile.

It is not a question of measurement or no measurement. The Ancient World could measure better than we can (witness Greek architecture as distinct from our own depressing dog kennels), so much as the Greeks saw measurement as an extension of metaphysics.[21] We have lost this integrated part of Tillyard's Elizabethan world picture, and thus the participants at this Pentagon press conference wander around like lost souls with bits of "concrete" measurement in one hand and bits of "mystical" belief in the other. That both number and measurement are indeed as mystical as anything else, and can indeed represent spirit, harmony and mystical experience[22] were thoughts gone from most of the garage-minds present at the press conference.

Wisely, Samford very quickly shifts the ground, and changes the entire axis of the argument. What he says now has nothing to do with Descartes, harmony or number:

> Our real interest in this project is not one of intellectual curiosity, but is in trying to establish and appraise the possibility of a menace to the United States. [23]

Since the conclusion of the Air Force was that UFOs posed no threat to the United States, this put the people of the United States in a very peculiar position. Let us suppose that when a family sits down for dinner each night, quite often a man walks through the dining room and disappears through a wall. Since this man appears to be quite a nice man, and shows no interest in or violent intention towards the family, they eat in peace and decide to take no notice. Thus do they manage the event and integrate the utterly fantastic into the mundane scheme, even though this event is acausal. They make the man and his actions invisible by reprogramming their cognitive responses, knowing full well that this liminal event had no connection with known economic or social *schema*. The single consideration of the absence of violence is the key to what is seen, recognised and interpreted, and what is not. The need to ask about the quantitive and qualitative structure, the nature and characteristics of the event, is obliterated as if by a surgical operation.

Strange? Yet this is virtually the answer one would get from the USAF if one were to write to them asking about Air Force UFO investigations in 2004.

The UFOs pose no threat.

The next part of the combination punch shows Samford trying to be far more clever, a dangerous thing for a man like him to attempt, and inevitably he makes a complete hash of it. He decides to answer a reporter in terms of the vexed question of the theoretical simultaneity of physical events, a somewhat abstract consideration for any press conference. Suddenly his argument is on the thinnest of thin ice, as he goes from a considering the non-threatening nature of an anomalous event to considering the concept of infinity, no less. Chieftain Cabell was never like this. But Chieftain Samford shows that he is prepared to do almost anything at all to deny the reality of the UFO, whose "acceptance," and "reality," as we have seen on other occasions, appears to be almost entirely dependent upon a form of words.

The very interstices of the perception of modern techno-industrial person are here. In one instance during the Washington sightings, three radars overlapped certainly; they were coupled with pilot visuals (civilian and military in this case), and also reported domestic radio interference (presumably on medium wave), and also ground observers took still photographs of saucer shaped objects in the night sky above the White House!

But the validity of all this depends, according to Samford, on our concept of simultaneity. Perhaps never in the history of aviation have strands of anthropology, sociology and indeed theology appeared in such an intriguing form and combination. We have a tribal leader, a very stressed human group, and theoretical concepts worthy of a Vatican Council meeting to judge the visions of St. Bernadette, or the legitimacy (a good Fortean replacement for "truth") of the involuntary levitations of St. Teresa of Avila. Since Einstein had long demolished space-time simultaneity some forty years before this press conference, no wonder some of those assembled had difficulty with this idea as expressed by Samford. When asked about overlapping radars, these electromagnetic emanations become almost an angel's wings:

Phenomena has passed from one radar to another and with a fair degree of certainty that it was the same phenomena…Now, when we talk about down to the split second, I don't know…

When asked soon afterwards about the operator's observations at the time of simultaneous registrations, this time Samford replies not in terms of difficult complexities, but in terms of plain silliness. We have to remind ourselves that the person speaking here is the Director of Intelligence of the Air Force of the United States as he passes from Einstein to ducks:

SAMFORD: Well, I could discuss possibilities. The radar screen has been picking up things for many years that — well birds, a flock of ducks. I know there's been one instance in which a flock of ducks was picked up and was intercepted and flown through as being an unidentified phenomenon.

PRESS: Where was that, General?

SAMFORD: I don't recall where it was. I think it might have been in Japan.

From a no-threat consideration, to simultaneity, to half-forgotten ducks (possibly in Japan), it is obvious that the General's technical concentration is lacking. He takes the situation as it comes at him and, improvising on the spot, does the very best he can, such as when he considers what is meant by the mass of a body. Here he reveals a lack of knowledge of school textbook science that represents a classic sixth form howler, unfortunately not picked up by anyone in the audience. Samford appears not to know that $w = mg$, where w = weight, m = mass, and g = the acceleration due to the Earth's gravity (about 32ft/second). If there is no appreciable gravity (such as in outer space), then there is almost zero mass, which is why the astronauts are seen floating inside their space vehicles. But of course this has absolutely no effect on the reflection back of electromagnetic waves from a molecular object in space, such as the body of an astronaut. Thus things almost without mass (gas, cloud vapour) can give solid returns.[24] Yet, says the General:

You know what no mass means — there's nothing there.

As par for the course, Samford adds the extraordinary concept of large, slow birds near enough to the aerial to give a significant blip:

> ...you would not get a blip as large as that from a bird. Unless it was close.

Again the General's physics are awry. Any bird, either large or slow, coming "close" to a static or moving antennae hosing out hundreds of watts of microwave energy would be fried, and more than Kentucky style.

It is a knockabout Punch and Judy show of bad science, loose thinking and ill-organised conspiracy within the shaky stage-flats of the PR game. The hapless Captain Roy James, the radar expert laughed at by Ruppelt, grows increasingly uneasy and evasive as his pathetic whimpers about "weather" fall apart, and several times he has to be rescued by the only slightly more adroit Samford. However, the General comes yet another cropper on the subject of guided missiles, of all things, about which he appears to know nothing at all.

As a pre-war seat-of-the-pants flier, Samford should have been, above all, conscious of fuel and range. The best and latest airborne technology is no good if the tank is dry. It is surprising therefore that Samford, and indeed many others at this time, thought seriously about UFOs being possible Russian guided missiles, the word "guided" being used very loosely during these years, even by Ruppelt himself. In addition, these possible missiles roam the US at will, exhibiting the most extraordinary behaviour in the most extraordinary conditions. They do all this (apparently) with tanks of gas (solid or liquid) that never appear to empty.[25]

So what is Samford referring to?

When we ask such a question, we must be aware that the old fraud and scoundrel called the *real* can produce as many numberless boxes of scandalous tricks as skunk-smoke when it is being hunted down. Here, the evidence for the "real existence" of the UFO is far greater than the evidence for the "real existence" of the said guided missiles. The difference is that the mystery of the super-missile is under control; the hive group can run it as a kind of limitless SF game in their heads. No matter how fantastic is this super-missile, it is born nevertheless of known scientific methods, and industrial and design procedures, and is a thing born of humanity. This minimal-evidence missile game is therefore given sanction if only because it has roots. But it really doesn't matter how much evidence is given for the "real existence" of the UFO, since it cannot be run in the same way because its performance spectrum has no knowable finite roots, it being a liminal object.

These differentials represent the internal structure of the paradigm. Here are the blood and bones of the smoke and mirrors, to mix a metaphor. As a tribal vanishing technique, "reality" in Samford's terms is defined by quantitive measurement, but *only* that quantitive measurement which has historical precedent. In this respect, Samford's definition of what constitutes a "qualified observer" is interesting. A pilot, says Samford, may see something most extraordinary, but if he cannot measure (i.e. put in an historical context) some aspect of it, he is not a qualified observer. Thus evidential scaling is limited to a certain style and form. In other words we are dealing with measurement governed by staging and presentations in cultural time matched against a something (the UFO) that does not appear to be born of known cultural time.

With some very slight alterations, and trapped with the necessary ornamentation, as a Vatican Council statement, all this takes some beating.

Flow of measured days and hours is one way of looking at time, but time as a flow of culture and ideas obeys no such law. Time in this sense can reverse itself; for instance, we have fallen far behind the Greeks of sixth century Athens, say, in many important matters. Also, two states of time may be present simultaneously, witness a possible conversation between Shakespeare and Francis Bacon, who was almost certainly in Shakespeare's audience at one time or another. In this impressionistic sense of time, General Samford is a late Victorian. Had the author Lytton Strachey lived to the 1950s, and had the wit to realise that the Industrial Revolution had taken place, Samford might have made it to Strachey's famous book, *Eminent Victorians*, and he might therefore have been judged alongside Ruskin and Dr. Arnold of Rugby as a symbol of the times. Samford's avoidance of what he calls metaphysics reflects the same doubts as Cardinal Manning had before he took the path to Rome.

Thus the aeroplanes, the atomic weapons, the technology, all the new developments are rooted in the fears of the almost-immediate European past, with all its doubts and uncertainties and leaps into the dark. This gives a whole new meaning to the phrase *deep background*.

With a few obvious edits in his acquired vocabulary, such as "radar," what Samford is saying could (and would) have been said by any well-educated Victorian such as Conan Doyle, and the points about the fallacies and faults of human observation made by Samford are almost out of the mouth of Sherlock Holmes. Indeed, Samford's surprising references to Mesmer, mind-reading and spiritualism[26] would have been grist to Holmes' mill, being an essential part of some of the major socio-cultural themes of the greater part of the nineteenth century.

We thus have many ghosts present here at this press conference, as many ghosts as were once in the spiritualist parlours of the prosperous Victorian middle class. The concepts of immateriality, for instance, so easily tossed about by Samford, are virtually the same concepts as discussed by the spiritualists and founders of the Society for Psychical Research. At times indeed we imagine at this press conference the UFO itself as being one of those women psychics, bound to a chair, ectoplasm pouring from her nose, her legs held by a Professor of Physics, her head grasped by a Professor of Mathematics, her arms held by two more Professors of Biology and Philosophy, and all to prevent supposed cheating! Seen now in brown speckled photographs, these savants (all of whom look as if they had a measuring tape stuck in a painful place) look like nineteenth century ghosts themselves. Caught and frozen in time by bright photo-powder flash and sepia tints, their heavy black drapes represent the stifling impostures of their own disciplines, judged to be more real than those of the psychic herself.

Science in youth and age, as always, is the most wonderful Fortean psychodrama.

Thus — though the powder-flashes, the heavy black drapes and the bound women are gone — the UFO mystery is still somewhat ectoplasmic. Instead of the tragic faces of Darwin and other bearded seers and sages embedded within the mess, we have the icons of technology, equally as tragic as the tortured faces of nineteenth century philosophy and science.

In this respect, a remarkable photograph was taken at the Samford press conference.[27] The mid tones of this picture have gone almost, it being a copy of many other copies of copies over the years. But the heavy black drapes of the Victorian séance have appeared perhaps for a last historical bow, and it looks very much as if the picture was taken by the powder-flash photography of days of yore. Ruppelt, at the back of Samford, has a nervous smile and looks as if he is keeping very much out of the way. Roy "Weather" James is at Samford's side, wearing an ingratiating grin. Seated at the side of Samford, looking up at him like a supplicant looking up at the face of Christ, is none other than General Ramey, Mr. "Roswell switched evidence" himself.

The Roswell alien crash/recovery story was buried for over thirty years before Stanton Friedman and others dug it out.[28] If Friedman is right (and this author thinks he almost certainly is) then this makes the man seated on Samford's right hand one of the greatest liars of history, to rank alongside Dr. Goebbels, Joseph Stalin, and the US President who did not know what a sex act was. It also implicates Samford himself in this monstrous conspiracy with the certainly unknowing Ruppelt as an innocent dupe. So whatever are the points made at this conference, whatever little information there is imparted, whatever the opinions expressed, Ramey's monstrous shadow falls over all and everything said, done, concluded and reported. The scale of the Big Lie in this case is not national, or international; it is cosmic, historical, and frankly unforgivable. That alien bodies were found but concealed is not only America's shame, but also the shame of all American authority, institutions, and everything America stands for.

Of course if Ramey knew, then Samford knew.

But Samford, sitting alongside possibly the biggest liar since Josef Goebbals, Minister for Nazi Propaganda, gives a Kafka-Orwellian answer fit to demolish all intellectual resistance in the manner of the coming age of TV commercials:

> There is no validity in individual sightings to mean any particular thing.

That this prime time cretinism comes from Head of Intelligence for the US Air Force is not only astonishing, it connects historically Pearl Harbor with 9/11. From Pearl Harbor to 9/11, the US is hopeless at detecting murderous threats.

In true nineteenth century fashion again, Samford christens the UFO "phenomena" and refers to it as such throughout the conference, "phenomena" being a word the Victorians would have loved. Again, this "phenomena" is a kind of ectoplasm (note the modern term "plasma," which is the idea of "etheric vapour" brought up to date, rather like the Victorian concept of the "ether," long abandoned by physics).

Thus do the public relations and stage-sets change in the drama of the never-ending argument between Matter, Mind and Spirit. Samford says "I am not a metaphysician," but never have Mind, Mechanism and Metaphysics come together in such a neat mid-twentieth century public relations form. The following statement by Samford could be from a possible book entitled *Kafka meets George Orwell*. It shows that whilst poor Samford had no great grasp of technology he had, certainly, bureaucratic skills of a wondrous kind. The following is a perfect example of a techno-tribal vanishing technique, and compares well with Orwell's idea of Newspeak and Kafka's story, *Investigations of a Dog*:

> You can investigate, but the technique of investigating a process of mind reading, for example, or the technique of investigating

the process of mesmerism. You can say will you investigate those things? I think probably we know no more about mind reading than the technique of investigating that [he is referring to pilot's observation], or the technique of investigating evidences of spiritualism than we do about these fields but for many years the fields of spiritualism had these same things in it in which completely competent credible observers reported incredible things. I don't mean to say that this is that sort of thing, but it's an explanation of an inability to explain and that is with us.[29]

This admission of his "inability to explain" is one of Samford's rare moments of concentration and intellectual honesty. But then he collapses again. He refers to "reports":

Let's take any one of these reports and pull it out and say, "Well what is the meaning of that one report?" None of these things in the period of our entire experience with them has had any validity on its own. The only thing that we hope for is to find enough similarity in sequence of these things so that you can begin to pull something out. There is no validity in them as individual sightings to mean any particular thing.[30]

In other words, we are not talking here about existence or non-existence so much as about *frequency* of occurrence, as yet another allowability vector with the paradigm, as regards the construction of the "real." The "real" as defined by frequency is now a vital element in the structure of the real. The discussion now enters a very interesting stage. Prior to this moment, the "real" had to be measurable. Now it has also to be *frequent*. This frequency consideration means that the ground is shifting. Frequency implies that at least something (the "phenomena") here considered has a rate of repetition, as distinct from not being in existence in the first place. Samford is manoeuvring; going from certainty to statistics. But almost immediately after this complaint about lack of frequency, comes the word "many."

PRESS: General, did you notice in all of your say, twenty per cent of the unexplainable reports a consistency as to colour, size, or estimated speed?

SAMFORD: None whatsoever.

PRESS: None whatsoever?

SAMFORD: No.

PRESS: Have you ever tracked the speed by radar of any particular object that you can explain?

SAMFORD: There have been many radar reports giving speed.

PRESS: What do they range from, sir?

SAMFORD: They range from zero to fantastic speeds.

Wow! And the final conclusion of this press conference was that the Washington sightings were due to temperature inversions! Now you see it, now you don't — not only is this stage performance country, this is an essay in which the goal posts are moving so fast they can be hardly seen, like a temperature inversion moving at supersonic speeds - apart, that is, from when it is standing still, or accelerating, illuminating, flashing colour-changes, and performing fantastic manoeuvres in the night sky above Washington, all registered by three radars and civilian/pilot observations. With weather like this, Washington should be so lucky!

This extraordinary weather is a stage-set at least equal to the cultural frauds of the Russian bomber stage-set, the B-36, star Capella, planet Venus, and the later "swamp gas" stage-sets.

Keyhoe in *Flying Saucers from Outer Space* gives us an era-shot of the end of the conference. He corners Samford, and asks him:

How big an inversion, General — how many degrees — is necessary to produce the effects at Washington Airport, assuming they're possible at all?

Samford looks at Keyhoe with no change in expression. Keyhoe adds that he would not want to play poker with this General. Samford replies in typical non-informative mode:

Well I don't know exactly. But there was an inversion.

Keyhoe then pressures him a little:

Do you know how many degrees, on either night?

But just as if this pair are playing out a B-Feature drama, someone breaks in sharply to protect the experimental alien, as it were, who may slip out of sync at any one time. This alien-supervisor comes in the form of Lieutenant Colonel Dewitt Searies and he eyes Keyhoe (not a popular figure with the Air Force) with suspicion, sneering at him in an almost insulting fashion:

You still in on this saucer business?

Before Keyhoe can reply, Searies turns to Samford:

Any time you're ready, sir; the newsreel men are waiting.

The B-Feature films themselves of course were not created from nothing. They originated from observation of such moments and personalities. Such moments indeed are common experience, and whilst they last, we surely think that we are made of the switched Escher-Penrose states discussed previously. Human consciousness at such times reveals itself as a pure function of programmed responses tailored to the requirements of a wider agenda, of which the sleepy Samford is a pure function. In films, these quickly switched modes of character and personality, motivation and mood can be brilliant entertainment, and some masterpieces of the genre have been created. But in the world outside films, such an experience can be far more disturbing, since without entertainment as a buffer we can hardly distance the experience. To suddenly see, through a sudden failure of concentration that a person we are speaking to belongs to another world, and goes back temporarily to it as if searching for momentarily "lost" instructions, is very disturbing. It is even more frightening to think that the world they go back to is listening to mutual responses and switching their host on and off according to pre-set programmes, paradigms and deep laid plots in Matter, Spirit, and Ideas.

Reinforcing this effect, as soon as Keyhoe turns from Samford, he meets Ruppelt himself for the first time, and introduces himself to this "broad-shouldered young officer with a disarming grin." But anyone expecting a sparkling exchange of ideas between two fascinating personalities will be disappointed. Ruppelt only discusses Keyhoe's fiction, avoiding all questions about his work on the UFO.

Thus significantly, the curtain is coming down on any radical questioning. It is coming down within big systems of the Western techno-industrial process, and it is coming down as regards discussions between two men like this. The world as prophesied by Kafka and Orwell (and indeed Wells and Huxley) is here; evolving programmes with agendas of their own have shut down both Ruppelt and Keyhoe in this instant. Like Samford, being momentarily almost dead in the existential sense, they cannot speak. Processing has shut their mouths as surely as if they were taped. Bank after bank of switching information arrays have rendered them mentally null and void, as much as if their tongues have been cut out.

Should any one doubt the full meaning of the concept of *conspiracy* then let them see it in action here in this non-moment between Keyhoe and Ruppelt. It is a conspiracy moreover that has both implicit and explicit vectors. The explicit element is the burgeoning influence of the CIA in UFO affairs, and the implicit element can be seen in terms of what happens between Ruppelt and Keyhoe. Had Jean Paul Sartre (still very much alive at this time) taken a look at this situation (though unfortunately not a single European intellectual ever did), he would have recognized living characters straight from the pages of his major work, *Being and Nothingness*. Blended with Orwell's idea of Newspeak, the reduction of language to mere mechanical responses of the basic industrial process is totally successful here: Keyhoe and Ruppelt are prisoners reduced to silence, the ultimate state of the life-long prisoner of the military industrial complex which is Goethe's *Leidstadt*, Eliot's *Wasteland*, and the Corporation rolled into one.

Confusions, Confessions and Almost Retractions

AFTER THE PRESS CONFERENCE, Ruppelt makes a brave effort to defend his hapless chief:

> General Samford made an honest effort to straighten out the Washington National Sightings [sic], but the cards were stacked against him before he started. He had to hedge on many answers to questions from the press because he didn't know the answers. This hedging gave the impression that he was trying to cover up something more than just the fact that his people had fouled up in not fully investigating the sightings.[31]

But immediately after the last sentence, he then goes on from this between-the-lines irony to an almost direct accusation of conspiracy:

> Then he [General Samford] had brought in Captain Roy James from ATIC to handle all the queries about radar.

146

He continues, but this time with heavier sarcasm, pointing out that vital witnesses were absent. James, who had just arrived in Washington that morning, was being asked to comment on the Washington sightings, about which he knew almost nothing and cared even less:

> James didn't know very much more about the sightings than he'd read in the papers. Major Dewey Fournet and Lieutenant Holcomb, who had been at the airport during the sightings, were extremely conspicuous by their absence, especially since it was common knowledge they weren't convinced the UFOs picked up on radars were weather targets.[32]

As distinct from the "honest effort" Ruppelt described above, this is an almost direct accusation of conspiracy to deceive. Ruppelt is showing some confusion, always the sign of mental and physical exhaustion.

But the cover-up brought

> exactly the result that was intended — the press got off our backs. Captain James's [sic] about the possibility of the radar targets being caused by temperature inversions had been construed by the press to mean that this was the Air Force's answer, even though today [Ruppelt was writing in 1956] the twin [Washington] sightings are still carried as unknowns.

The next morning headlines "from Bangor to Bogota" read:

> AIR FORCE DEBUNKS SAUCERS AS JUST NATURAL PHENOMENA.[33]

But perhaps we have done an injustice to Samford. Perhaps he was far cleverer than ever we thought. One thing was certain that concerns Ruppelt: Samford, clever or nor, was out to trash him good. After being promised far greater support, Ruppelt found that Project Blue Book was gradually being scaled down. Just before he left for civilian life in late 1952, Project Blue Book was again down to a staff of only two men, this being reduced to one man again very soon afterwards. Who replaced Ruppelt? Their names and faces are now almost erased from history; this hardly matters because they were time-servers, mediocrities and conformists, these road blocks representing the way that the corporation does things.

Something has happened to our hero. He is losing his concentration and his confusions multiply. Different planes of reference become twisted and self-cancelling as he tries desperately to find black and white terms in a greyscale world that has grown rather too complicated for him, a world in which he is all at sea:

> The Washington National Sightings proved one thing, something that many of us already knew: in order to forestall any more trouble similar to what we had just been through we always had to get all of the facts and not try to hide them. A great deal…

Trying to hide facts? Who was trying to hide facts, the entire Samford apparatus? With this level of simian duplicity Ruppelt shows that he is not only exhausted, he is out of his depth. As a boy scout he has grown up rather too quickly into a world become too complicated for him.

As such, he is now beginning to smell rats in all kinds of places. For instance, he finds that somebody or something has been pressuring many vital witnesses, who appear to have changed their statements after the event.

Here then, is our hero confronting his first suspicions that, like Kafka's Josef K, he exists within a facade: a stage-set whose flats can be moved any which way. He is beginning to realize the painfully obvious: that General Samford put his brains and energy (what little the poor fellow had of these virtues) into the vanishing of the UFO as distinct from evaluating the "evidence." Indeed the evidence becomes irrelevant: the UFO, as a liminal form, cannot be *allowed* rather than be evaluated as a false or true thing.

In such a manner were both media time and media truth born in the post-war world.

Ruppelt's bravery and honour, his simplicities, national and political, intellectual and practical, are about to trash him but good. General Samford as American Military Authority is about to turn into a lizard, B-Feature style. In his comparatively short time in UFO research Ruppelt has not only matured, he has mutated in media time. As we have seen, it all started in innocence and not a little fun. At the beginning of his journey into experience, all that was really required was a separating out of fact from fiction. This might well be a hard thing to do, thought our hero, but at least it was a well tried operational technique that always looked and sounded impressive. One could score Brownie points and much praise from the sane and the sensible for ostensibly separating out the facts from the fictions. But unfortunately for our hero, and unlike anyone else around him, he has some spark of a first-class brain and for such, the world is far too complicated a place for it to be constructed of facts, on the one hand, and fictions on the other. He is starting to see through some of screens around him, and it is doing him no good at all.

There comes a point for all heroes when fact and fiction change place. After the Samford press conference it is as if Ruppelt knows that his time is limited, and the doors of Blue Book (and many other doors in the American mind) are about to close forever. The world he entered has now become a baffling, complex place where the UFO itself has become a thing bound by high-level conspiracies whose boundaries stretch to infinity. He is in a prototypical *Matrix*.

Now he sees that someone or something has been going around behind everyone's back snuffing out candles. Under "interrogation" (Ruppelt's word), the "large fiery-orange-coloured sphere" seen by the radar operators at Washington National has been reduced to "merely a star." It is a truly Fortean moment: the information is being re-scaled in order that the experience becomes manageable. The operators said that on the night in question they had become merely "excited." As Charles Fort would say, it must have been some considerable excitement because, as Ruppelt notes, according to astronomical charts there were no exceptionally bright stars where the UFO was seen over the range station. He adds:

> And I heard from a good source that the tower men had been 'per-shaded' a bit.

Well good readers, that is a genuine piece of vintage night side America, if you please. Here is another: regarding the second F-94 interception, the pilot, after giving both Ruppelt and the press his story about vainly trying to intercept unidentified lights, said in an official report that all he saw was a ground light reflecting off a layer of haze. Ruppelt, trying to rally his shaken confidence in himself as an impartial observer amidst some very partial candle-snuffers, mentions as a "negative" point that the three (overlapping) radars registered a simultaneous contact *only once*. We might ask ourselves how many times does he or anybody else need? Here is our old friend *frequency* again, and here are the figures Ruppelt gives for the Washington incidents alone:

> We found out that the UFOs frequently visited Washington. On May 23 fifty targets had been tracked from 8:00 PM till midnight. They were back on the Wednesday between the two famous Saturday-

night sightings, the following Sunday night, and the night of the press conference; then during August they were seen eight more times. On several occasions military and civilian pilots saw lights where the radar showed the UFOs to be.[34]

How high a frequency must we have for acceptance?

The question is difficult to answer, because the culture, the corporations and the paradigm are grounding the oscillations, filtering the signal, or defending the high strategic passes of the old Empire.

The only freedom we have is one choice of metaphor.

At some point in the ritual journey of initiation of all warriors and heroes, there comes a stage in the *mysterium* where the beloved facts and fiction of intellectual childhood swap roles, one becoming the other. The separations of innocence and experience are not clear anymore. Ruppelt was not a well-educated man of the middle class. He did not have a broad liberal education to give him many alternative psycho-cultural options, and the Air Force and everything it represented to American society was certainly something of a father figure to him, as indeed it was for the pre-Vietnam generations. But the father (Samford and Authority) has been caught with his greasy fingers in the greasy till of belief-manipulation. Father has let Ruppelt down, and he is starting to see a very different Air Force and a very different America, and the end of the line is visible, both for himself and for Operation Blue Book.

He comes out of his visit to Magonia (where all objects are Escher-Penrose objects) and falls apart. The liminal object of the UFO, and all it relates to, starts to shred just like a newspaper under heavy rain. Watching over the years that have passed, we see the stories come apart as little bits go missing...

The Air Force, the rank, uniform, the pace and breadth of life and mission, all fall apart, leaving him full of excuses, qualifications and retractions. Frankly, Ruppelt is in a bit of a mess.

Project Blue Book is verbally and, hence conceptually, erased in an operation that any hard-line Soviet commissar of the time would have admired. Names and faces disappear, the stories come apart, hang together as threads and webs as little bits go missing. Thus the American corporation and the Russian Soviet were united by tribal rituals far older than the rocks upon which they sat.

Ruppelt was a caring, incorruptible, wonderful man, and his caring for America and the Air Force, and everything those entities represented to him, may have helped aggravate the heart condition that caused his death in 1960.

Appendix

Deconstruction of the B-29

LET US DO SOMETHING that we are not much encouraged to do these days.

Let us try and rediscover the power of one of the great banned faculties of the twentieth century: the Imagination.

Imagine a B-29 bomber crashed long ago on an island in the Solomons group.

Like Princess Diana and Elvis Presley, the B-29 wreck has reached the regions of that advanced life form called pure information. We can be sure that for the islanders, the crashed Superfortress will enter the mythological pantheon of universal advertisements, just as the UFO itself has done for the people that have long since moved on to make the very different "improved" wings of very different aeroplanes to the B-29. The idea of "improvement" of course is, like Rationalism, a very late and rather callow arrival on the historical scene. The concept of getting better relates to very rapid industrial class-change rather more than anything else. The idea of improvement, either sociological or technological, means managing the nature and targets of ever-young Product Time and its latest development, the showbiz politics of promise-control, from Five Year Plans to Mars Bars, from Monica Lewinski to Dark Matter.

Imagine.

The haunted fuselage of this crashed sample of Product Time comes from our almost-recent past, but now to the islanders, it is a past as far back as Pyramid Time.

WITHIN THE RUST and grease and analogues of the fractured shapes of the wrecked bomber are interwoven the plots of both consumerism, technology and the mystique of change. Here in this alien artifact are the long dead crew, most of them victims of the 20mm Shigeru cannon of a supercharged Zero coming fast out of the Pacific sun one early morning in May 1945. Here, still in flying suits and life jackets covered with yellow dust from cannon-burst bags of shark-repellent, are shinbones and vertebrae from Miami, Little Rock, and Texas. There, rusting headphones still cling to shot-up skulls from New York and San Francisco; here, broken legs, necks and backbones from New Orleans, Baton Rouge and Philadelphia, still sit upright before controls, radio sets and an array of navigating equipment built, tested, and almost paid for in Detroit, Memphis and Idaho.

Before this broken lance of the vanguard nation, stand the ranks of a worshipping congregation. They listen intently to a dancing and chanting Magic Man who whirls a bamboo-stick before the cracked Perspex nose of that essay in wonder and danger that is the Boeing B-29. This is the entrance to the shrine. In the back row of our congregation, let us imagine a pair of eyes that avoid the Magic Man's gaze, and look rather more discursively into the silent ruins of the torn-off Wright Cyclone engines.

Let us say these are the eyes of Hero.

Hero avoids the Magic Man's concern with the great chiefs buried in these ruined pyramid-chambers of broken American aluminium, for Hero is experiencing instant Natural Selection. He has begun to replace all Magic Man concerns by quite another kind of question, and we can reconstruct a moment in which that great white hope of humanity called rationalism is born.

The dancing and chanting finish. Night comes, and taking care to avoid the Magic Man, Hero pays a secret visit to the depths of the temple. By the light of a shrouded pig-grease candle, there is revealed inordinate beauty and form. Hero asks himself new questions as his fingers and eyes move over the shapes and surfaces of thousands of old American dreams. Unable to avoid his eternal present, he examines products and techniques long gone with the America of Glenn Miller's orchestra. How do they do *this?* How do they do *that?* Hero does not know that a half century after the crash, that in many cases, "they" have forgotten the techniques by means of which they did this and that.

Hero moves from new gods to old technologies as he surveys precise angles, neat joints, and smooth shapes. He touches textures and shapes of Vulcanised rubber and Bethlehem Mayari low-alloy steel; he passes by wiring, castings and very early plastics (of varying quality), from Seattle, Chicago and Los Angeles. Through the complexity of the shattered instrumentation; carefully he moves past the 50. cal turret, discarded parachutes, half-inflated dinghies and oxygen masks. The dregs of long dried brake fluid and carbonised rubber come to him as a mid-century techno-industrial Proustian *Madeleine*: Paxolin, Bakelite and Celluloid, all incense rising in praise to the lost gods of apple-pie America: Chance-Vought, Curtiss, Northrop, and Convair; Bell, Tesla and Edison.

On this night, all are present as Hero moves through this broken lance of the vanguard nation. Passing early radar vacuum tubes, fuel-tanks, and still-full bomb racks, Hero will become aware of the extent of a conspiracy beyond all his imagining. He will begin to understand a little of the mythology of the techno-industrial solution as represented by the aircraft, now long gone as Bob Hope's America. He will begin a new experience of Time not as the coming and going of sun, moon and tide, but Time as ideological quanta pulsating between Plan, Product and Performance.

As a first experimental cerebral, Hero will begin a journey of initiation through the rites of Industrial passage: principles of operation, purpose and manufacture will permeate his very being. In this shattered temple of a fuselage, he is being painfully re-birthed. On his voyage of discovery he will often wish he had stayed with the rattling skulls of the tribal sorcerer, and continue to think and accept that the hydraulic fluid seeping from a shattered brake-drum are the grotto-tears of some dying animal, sorrowing for mankind.

Hero will want to know the "facts" that he has no doubt heard talk of from missionaries and visiting anthropologists, from whom, intuitively, the crashed B-29 has been carefully concealed for fifty years. He will try to jump out of his loincloth paradigm by attempting that celebrated process of stage-management called demystification. But from the B-29 to the F-117 Stealth aircraft is a long journey again into a mythological world text. Before he goes on that forward journey, Hero will have to learn to read backwards, although he may not be familiar with either textual dimension. He will have to travel back in time through many centuries of sleepwalking experiments with temperatures, pressures, alignments, tooling, finishing, fitting and design, and on the way will see bankruptcies, suicides, madness, and not a little love and dedication.

Hero does not realise that the Magic Man knows what is happening. He can see inside Hero's head. He does not do or say anything. He knows from the way Hero looked at the aeroplane that he has already begun a great epic journey. The Magic Man knows that in his new task of trying to understand, Hero will have to travel back from the B-29 to the struts of the Wright Flyer, to the Colt pistol and Gatling machine-gun men of the Civil War, back to the English blacksmiths who first hot-hammered the crude-forged iron straps round the parched water barrels of the arriving *Mayflower*.

He knows that Hero will have to struggle with the pre-Newtonian puzzles about momentum and acceleration, mass and pressure, and will have to re-discover Pythagoras, Archimedes and Aristotle. Beyond them lies the open hearth furnace, its stone cups boiling with bronze, and all surrounded by cursing and hope, despair, defeat and victory, birth, death and dream.

Off the main roads of the central mystery, there are numberless side turnings in the shape of questions: on what dismal cold morning did the outline of that particular decision form? What was so and so doing at the time? Was there a particular night on which the curve of a cheek became the shape of an aeroplane? All the mistakes, guesses and approximations of all these days and nights will feed back on themselves, providing interpretation as crazy as anything in our own science or religion. An ever evolving landscape of belief turns the fuselage into a grail-vessel. Matter decoded is pure dream, leading back to the cave mouth and Hycernian forest of other wrecked fuselages beyond the sun and moon.

When Hero comes full circle, the waiting magus will smile. What has Hero learned from his great journey? Perhaps he knows of the mysteries of the Fall in terms of a question: why do the gods need *machines* to fly? Why do they need *radios* to talk to people on other islands?

Perhaps nature does not experiment socially, choosing instead to concentrate upon certain individuals, such as Hero or George Adamski. The rest, like the animals, go on happily flapping and hooting, snorting and grunting to infinity. Perhaps that is why certain people lead shattered lives. To be "chosen" is to be the subject of some illimitable cosmic experiment. Just as we are about to award Frank Stranges and Adamski very low marks out of ten, we must remember that soon after their pan-dimensional texts were published, Flower Power hit California, the home of both Adamski and Stranges. After that the world was never the same again, and space folk were seen everywhere. Adamski's life-long obsession with Aetherian theosophy, which links almost every single one of these early saucer visionaries, had reached social melt down, and partly because of this development, the American army was later to be taken from the battlefields of Vietnam.

If such people have anything to teach us, it is not that the gods are good, bad or indifferent, but that they can manifest at all, that they can run riot like a cellular virus, sow their images in minds which become malls, and vice versa. They show us also that we ourselves have power to create that sacred and utterly scandalous tomfoolery, which is always at the heart of time, change and product.

Meantime, back in the bush, in a secret place unknown even to the Magic Man, Hero picks up a stone and starts to shape it into a B-29, whose robot being now exists as a broken Roswell Scroll in his head.

But far away in the deep forest, the Magic Man smiles.

He knows how far Hero has to journey before he frees the shape from the block.

Corporate Revisionism
The Extra Chapters of the Re-Written Book That Never Were

PRIOR TO WRITING *An American Demonology*, I found that many who wrote about Ruppelt emphasized strongly that the revised edition of *The Report on Unidentified Flying Objects,* published in 1959, contained an extreme negative reaction to the somewhat positive view on UFOs expressed in the first edition, which appeared in 1956. Upon obtaining a copy of this revised edition however, I was surprised to find that the situation was not quite as I had been led to believe.

The revised edition of 1959 contains three extra chapters added to the seventeen chapters of the original 1956 edition. Otherwise, the main body of the original text is unaltered. The first of the three new chapters, Chapter Eighteen, contains, no less, a totally positive reinforcement of Ruppelt's views. For example, I was most surprised to see in this chapter the reports of the gung-ho believer Leonard Stringfield presented uncritically, alongside the equally hair-raising reports of commercial pilots. You simply don't mention Leonard Stringfield of all people if you want to put down the UFO!

Another sample of Ruppelt's up-beat mood here, from this same chapter, is his brutal smashing down of the Air Force's attempt to cover up the 1956 sighting at the Hutchinson Naval Air Station:

A few days later the Air Force told the Kansans what they had seen: the reflection from burning waste gas torches in a local oil field. This was greeted by the Kansan version of the Bronx Cheer."[1]

This hardly matches with the pro-Air Force mood set in Chapter Twenty, and hardly equates with his wife Elizabeth's saying to researchers Hall and Connors that her husband was "deeply disappointed" by the Air Force expressing its disapproval of his book. However, by the way Ruppelt talked with mounting disgust and sarcasm about the Air Force throughout his book, and did not choose to change a word of this text when given the opportunity, do we really believe that he was "disappointed"?

He also shows his old form in the new Chapter Eighteen. He takes the side of NICAP against the Air Force, and gives a very positive view of a score or more of amazing UFO sightings during the latter part of 1957 and up to the end of 1958. These include sightings at Ellington AFB, Los Angeles, the Gulf of Mexico, the Los Alamitos Naval Air Station, Levelland, Texas, Danby, California, and also once again, the White Sands Missile range. He finishes this chapter by analysing an interceptor chase from Duluth Municipal Airport, and he dismisses weather, radar anomalies, atmospheric conditions and sightings of the planet Venus.

So far, so good.

The new Chapter Nineteen can be discounted, since it relates to Adamski,[2] Fry and Bethorum, the so-called UFO contactees, and since a negative view of such people was expressed by Ruppelt in the first edition, this new discussion does not count as any kind of alteration of view.

The only somewhat "negative" chapter is the final Chapter Twenty. Here, yes, we immediately detect a change. But this chapter consists of a little more than six scrappy pages, written in something of a hurry as compared to the carefully detailed two previous chapters. It has no weight, its superficial conclusions are rather flip and out of character, very much as if it were something of an add-on.

There are some very strange and mysterious shadows here. At this time the Cold War was at its height, and the iron grip of both the Soviet Union and Maoist China upon independent thinkers of every kind furnished many such add-on "confessions" as this. Many such were extracted under torture indeed, or at least under very severe mental and physical deprivation during which hypnosis, drugs and electric shocks were used to change the political view of dissenters; many of whom were then put on public trial in a zombie condition, such as Cardinal Mindzetny. We derive the term "brain washing" from this time. The Chinese interrogation methods practiced on US prisoners discussed in the novel *The Manchurian Candidate* also comes to mind as does Arthur Koestler's novel, *Darkness at Noon*. These books were written and many of the prophesised events came about in the 1950s, including Lee Harvey Oswald's journey to Russia and back to America, which must be one of the strangest journeys of all human history.

Whilst of course it would be absurd to suggest that Ruppelt had been under this high degree of pressure and high intrigue, this last Chapter Twenty does indicate, given the faltering style, that he was under some degree of pressure at least, as pointed out by Donald Keyhoe. It certainly reads like a revisionist attempt to re-write history as the old Communists would have understood it.

But the Communist interrogators were all more careful than this. By comparison, there is considerable evidence that not much thought was given to the detailed changes. For example, in this 1959 edition, there is no change or addition to the original foreword of 1956. A completely revised foreword or even a short additional paragraph could have brought the foreword in line with new views expressed in the last chapter. Also, the new 1959 edition carries the same date of publication (1956) as the previous edition, even though it was published some three years afterwards, in 1959! Since the book therefore hangs in indeterminate time and space, it has something of a liminal quality in itself! We know that the second edition was published in 1959, because in Chapter Nineteen Ruppelt discusses George Adamski's world tour, which took place during that year.

This carelessness is very strange and most uncharacteristic of both Ruppelt the man and the meticulous Doubleday editing staff, who were very pleased with the book and its sales and reception. There are other very odd things. In Chapter Twenty he repeats a story (the Dayton sightings of summer 1952) that he has already told previously in the body of the text. A good editor would have pointed out that repetition immediately.

Also in this last, suspect chapter, the Lubbock Lights are explained as "night-flying moths reflecting the bluish-green light of a nearby row of mercury vapour street lights." A Fortean gem of an explanation that is now a classic, along with swamp gas and earth lights. We also get some vintage stuff about the planet Jupiter, and a positive opinion about temperature inversions on radar being mistaken for UFOs. This kind of thing, when compared to his anger at such an explanation for the Washington sightings, makes Chapter Twenty look rather silly. There was only one way to bring off this retraction, and that was to revise completely the body of the text. Doubleday, in not asking him to do this, or not doing it for him, trashed the effect of the changed opinions of Chapter Twenty.

Thus the entire feel of this last chapter is that although most probably in part, at least, it originated from Ruppelt's hand, there is present an overlay of another rather inept editing hand. As a whole, Chapter Twenty lacks conviction, is rather hollow, and in my opinion is a bit of a paste-up. It looks and sounds as if someone not very experienced has tried to imitate Ruppelt's style and the result is a kind of queasy uncertainty, a rather phoney mix of direct statement and gnomic qualification not usual for Ruppelt. In comparison with the rest of the book, this extra chapter is an embarrassment. In any case, this action is a reminder of the significant document-burning cases mentioned in this book, and also the resignation of Hillenkoeter, a battlement-ghost of America if ever there was.

Of course, under pressure, he could have made these face-tearing retractions himself as scratches upon the cell walls of his life. He could have left them faulty as a deliberate act to show the world that his retractions were, like the UFO, and indeed like the solid globe itself, not quite real.

Notes

Prologue

1 See *The Enigma of Intelligence* by Andrew Hodges (Harper Collins, 1985).

2 See Keyhoe, *Saucers from Outer Space* (Universal-Tandem Publishing Co Ltd., 1970). pp 53, 100 and 107.

3 Edward J. Ruppelt, "The Report on Unidentified Flying Objects," Victor Gollancz, London, 1956, p 65. This fundamental source is hereinafter cited as "Ruppelt". See also UFO Intelligence Summary (Nuclear Connection Project) at [**w**] nicap.dabsol.co.uk/ncp-ufois.htm

4 See Stephan Bernath's *Top Secret* (Arcturus Books, 2003), pp 43–44 Bernath quotes Peter Gersten (1981): "Department of Defence, USAF, and CIA documents revealed that during October, November, and December of 1975, reliable military personnel repeatedly sighted unconventional aerial objects in the vicinity of nuclear weapons storage areas, aircraft alert areas, and nuclear missile control facilities at Loring Air Force Base, Maine; Wurtsmith Air Force Base, Michigan; Malmstrom Air Force Base, Montana; Minot Air Force Base, North Dakota; and Canadian Forces Station, Ontario. Many of the sightings were confirmed by radar. At Loring Air Force Base, the interloper 'demonstrated a clear intent on the weapons storage area.' An Air Force document says that 'Security Option III' was implemented and that security measures were coordinated with fifteen Air Force bases from Guam to Newfoundland."

5 See article by Donald A. Johnson *Do Nuclear Facilities Attract UFOs?* (*International UFO Reporter* Summer 2002 Vol 27, No 2, p 7).

6 See *Scientific Study of Unidentified Flying Objects* (Bantam Books, NY, 1969) by Dr. Edward U. Condon, Project Director. Introduction by Walter Sullivan. This was a report commissioned by the United States Air Force and conducted by the University of Colorado.

7 See *Early Flying Machines* by Charles Gibbs-Smith (Eyre Methuen London, 1975), and also *Visions of Spaceflight: Images from the Ordway Collection* by Frederick I. Ordway III (Publishers Group West, 2001).

8 Penguin, 2001.

A Chain of Being

1 *Ruin From the Air* (Hamish Hamilton, 1977) by Gordon Thomas and Max Morgan-Witts, p 427.

2 Michael David Hall and Wendy Ann Connors, "Captain Edward J Ruppelt, Summer of the Saucers

– 1952", 2000. This fundamental source is hereinafter cited as "Hall and Connors". Here, see Special Preface XIX.

3　See the MX-334 and MXP-1001 designs discussed in *Wings of Fame*, Vol 2.

4　This aircraft, the biggest aircraft ever to become operational, was a monstrous folly, completely left behind by the rapid pace of technological developments. It was Curtis LeMay's still-born child, called by some (who had more confidence than the crews), "The American Big Stick." Even on paper, it looked desperately old-fashioned for its time. Its airspeed was so low, in order to stop it being eaten alive by Migs, it had more gun-turrets stuck all over it than a porcupine has quills. To add insult to injury, the Air Force suggested that this aircraft carry a small parasite fighter under its belly, which theoretically, would hook back on to the massive bomber after an interception, presumably over Russian territory! This additional comic episode is well described in *Wings of Fame*, Vol 7. Finally, the last versions of the propeller-driven B-36 suffered the indignity of having four jet engine attached (two at the end of each wing) in order to increase its speed and take-off power.

5　A fully working Mig-15 was available only in 1953 long after Ruppelt had left Blue Book. It was tested in Okinawa by Chuck Yeager himself before being delivered to ATIC in that year.

6　A design whose unique suspension and sloped armour was copied by the Russians from a revolutionary pre-war tank prototype built by the American engineer J. Walter Christy. Of course, neither Britain nor America took any notice of Christy at the time. The Germans built the Panther to rival the T-34, and certainly the Panther influenced the design of the British Centurion tank, perhaps the most successful tank of all time, being in service in some armies over fifty years later.

7　The account in the Combat Diary 22 [**w**] www.combat-diaries.co.uk is a serialised version of the out of print 1995 (Midlands Publishing) Aerofax article *Lockheed Martin F-117 Nighthawk* by Jay Miller. This is quite the most astonishingly detailed treatment of design, construction and theory of stealth technology from the construction of the first flying model "Have Blue" in 1977 at Groom Lake, otherwise known as Area 51. Readers of this article might also be interested in the following remarks by Dr. Reimar Horton. These were made in 1950, only a few months before Ruppelt joined ATIC in early January, 1951: "As wooden surfaces offer very little reflection to electric waves, they are almost invisible on the radar screen. And as a fighter pilot should utilize the element of surprise to the full, especially at night, so should his aircraft be constructed of wood…" Here we have no less the first hint of an idea for the composite "stealth" material. Even earlier the British *Mosquito* twin-engine fighter was made almost entirely of wood. As a night-fighter, and high-speed intruder it was possibly the best

Notes

aircraft of WWII. Only the jet-powered Me 262 (at a pinch) proved equal to it.

8   See E. H. Cookridge *Gehlen Spy Of the Century* (Corgi 1972).

9   Office of Strategic Services Operative 1942–45, and CIA Director 1953–61.

10 For a full discussion of the various characters involved in the UFO "war" at ATIC during this time, see Hall and Connors.

11 For detailed information on Colonel Harold Watson's involvement with the Me 262, see chapter nine of Hugh Morgan's excellent and detailed book *Me 262 Stormbird Rising* (Osprey, Reed Consumer Books Ltd, 1994) with a foreword by Generalleutnant Adolf Galland, one of Germany's leading fighter aces.

12 See Anthony Samson *The Arms Bazaar* (Hodder and Stoughton, 1977) p 99.

13 *Yeager* (Arrow, New York, 1986) p 235.

14 Ruppelt, p 120

15 See this author's own book, *Politics of the Imagination*, given the Anomalist Award for Best Biography, 2002 (Headpress/Critical Vision, 2002) [**w**] www.headpress.com

16 Hall and Connors, p 27.

17 Ruppelt, p 121.

18 Ruppelt, p 122.

19 For an account of two other White Sands incidents of April 24, 1949, and November 3, 1957. See *The UFO Encyclopedia* by Margaret Sachs, p 364 (Corgi, 1981).

20 Ruppelt describes the old Project Grudge files as having been pulled out of filing cabinets and drawers and thrown into large storage bins.

21 Ruppelt, p 124.

22 *Aliens from Space* by Major Donald E. Keyhoe (Doubleday, 1975) pp 93–103.

23 Ruppelt, p 62.

24 Ruppelt, p 67.

25 *UFOs and the National Security State* (Keyhole Publishing Company, 2002).

26 See also Keyhoe's account of Hillenkoeter's resignation in *Aliens from Space* (Panther, 1975).

27 A grisly example of this is provided by a comment from a female member of the notorious Baader-Meinhoff gang who killed a German minister whilst fitting him with a pair of shoes in a shop. Whilst talking about the shoes non-stop, she produced a gun and shot him dead. He did not "see" the gun because of his intense concentration on what his killer was saying about the shoes. See *Hitler's Children* by Jillian Becker (Michael Joseph, 1977).

28 Since 1973, Roger Penrose has been the Rouse Ball Professor of Mathematics at Oxford. Said to be one of the world's greatest living mathematician, Penrose and his father are the creators of the famous Penrose staircase and the impossible triangle known as the tribar. Both of these figures were used in the work of Dutch graphic artist Maurits Cornelis Escher.

29 Maurits Cornelis Escher (1898–1972) was a Dutch artist most known for his woodcuts, lithographs and mezzotints, which tend to feature impossible constructions, explorations of infinity, and tessellations.

30 Ruppelt, p 126.

31 The official Air Force report

describing this encounter is Air Intelligence Information Report Number IR-3-51E prepared on September 21, 1951, by Director of Intelligence Lieutenant-Colonel Bruce K. Baumgardner. This report is reproduced in Timothy Good's *Beyond Top Secret* (1997, p 332).

32 Ruppelt, p 127.
33 Ruppelt, p 128.
34 Hall and Connors, p 57.
35 Hall and Connors, p 58.
36 Hall and Connors, p 46.
37 Ruppelt, p 129.
38 Hall and Connors, p 59.

A Set of Correspondences

1 Ruppelt, p 154.
2 This phrase is used (at least in Britain) by media folk to describe a broadcast programme that is so well balanced it is completely meaningless.
3 Ruppelt, p 155.
4 Ruppelt, p 157.
5 Ruppelt, pp 156–157.
6 Ruppelt, pp 157–158.
7 Ruppelt, p 156.
8 In November 1951, Samford had replaced Cabell as Air Force Intelligence Director. Cabell became what was then known as Director of the Joint Staff for the Joint Chiefs of Staff, becoming in 1953 the Deputy Director of the CIA.
9 Ruppelt, p 158.
10 "…by that time the distinction of developing the first stored-programme computer had fallen to another country — Babbage's homeland." (Stan Augarten, *Bit by Bit*, Houghton Mifflin Co., 1984.)
11 Ruppelt, p. 161.

12 Ruppelt, p 169.
13 Ruppelt, p 173.
14 Ruppelt, p 175.
15 Ruppelt, p 175.
16 Ruppelt, p 258.
17 Ruppelt, p 252.
18 Ruppelt, p 253.
19 Ruppelt, pp 20-21
20 Hall and Connors produce plenty of evidence that Watson was still around and exerting his anti-UFO influence from outside ATIC.
21 See [**w**] www.presidentialufo.com/wilbert_smith_lectures.html and also Dolan, *UFOs and the National Security State*, pp 146–147.
22 See Keyhoe, *Flying Saucers From Outer Space*, pp 130–151.
23 Ruppelt, p 175-176.
24 Ruppelt, p 175.
25 Ruppelt, p 175.
26 Ruppelt, p 175.
27 Dornberger set the work schedule by means of which 20,000 inmates at the Nordhausen concentration camp were worked to death. He entered the United States under Operation Paperclip (organized by US General Medaris) and became a senior executive of Bell Aerosystems of Textron.
28 (1905–85) For a short period in the middle 1950s Biot became involved with rocket radioguidance problems and the question of disturbance from ground reflections. To evaluate this effect he developed an original theory for the reflection of electromagnetic and acoustic waves from a rough surface, showing that the effect of the roughness may be replaced by a smooth boundary condition.
29 It must be borne in mind that Operation Blue Book was *supposed* to be a secret project.

Notes

30 Ruppelt, p 177.

31 Ruppelt, pp 177–178.

32 Ruppelt, p 178.

33 See [**w**] www.project1947.com/ fig/chilwhit.html and [**w**] www.usufocenter.com/ ufologist.html

34 Ruppelt, pp 188–189.

35 Ruppelt, p 199.

36 Ruppelt, p 188.

37 Keyhole Publishing, April 2000.

38 Wild Flower Press, 2003.

39 For details of the patchy radar coverage of the US at this time, see *A Century of Sightings* by Michael David Hall, pp 172–173.

40 Ruppelt, p 174.

41 Every experienced author knows that when a MSS is submitted to a publisher, and the editor says he or she is going to give it to someone else for further consideration, then the book is going to be rejected.

42 Ruppelt, p 518

43 Ruppelt, p 189.

44 See this author's article *High Moon* in *Fortean Times* 168.

45 Ruppelt, p 195.

46 Quoted by Hall and Connors, pp. 103–104, from a CUFOS report.

47 This idea was later abandoned. It was revived fifty years later by computerized automatic surveillance cameras recording the most peculiar things, such as lights appearing to "investigate" a building, and squirrels running at a recorded 60mph!

48 Ruppelt, p 201.

49 Ruppelt, p 205.

50 Ruppelt, p 207.

A Dance

1 Ruppelt, p 210.

2 *Countdown for Decision* (John B Medaris, Paperback Library Inc., 1960). See also *Nasa, Nazis & JFK* (David Hatcher Childress, Adventures Unlimited, 1996).

3 Medaris, p 49.

4 Even a very brief look at a catalogue of Russian bomber type aircraft of this period will confirm what Medaris is saying. There were no Russian strategic bombers worth the name in operational service, and very few on the design board. The very small number of large, long-range bomber types (such as the Tupelov Bear) were designed for strategic reconnaissance, long range sea patrols, and radar pickets. The Russians concentrated on fighter design, and tactical support aircraft for the Warsaw Pact armies, with types such as Beagle and Badger. Supersonic penetration of the American mainland by manned aircraft was of course out of the question if only because of range. Nevertheless, the American public were sold the completely false idea of a mass of very slow propeller-driven bombers droning in squadrons towards central American cities. Even if such old-fashioned squadrons had existed (and they did not), they would have been shot down like quail over Alaska and Canada by hundreds of modern jet fighters, such as the long-range Northrop Scorpion, designed for exactly this role. The idea was that the few Soviet bomber crews who happened to get through would face the unhappy prospect of a suicide mission, since they would not have had fuel to get back, fighting their way through yet

more fighters to their Russian bases, all of which would have been nuked in any case. How such a "penetration" scenario could have been constructed by sane men is a good question. Nevertheless, the American public believed it, and built air-raid shelters.

Folklore researchers would be interested in what appears to be two modern techno-myths tangled up with one another: the Intercontinental Ballistic Missile (which *would* have been effective) and the residual memory of WWII bombers. We thus have a very interesting situation from the psycho-social point of view: the citizens know they cannot defend themselves against ICBMs, so they are going through the motions of defending themselves against something they know about but which nevertheless did not exist! A good Fortean equation, that. The military would not enlighten the public. They themselves believed what their own fears told them. Thus an amazing modern industrial fantasy was made complete by the design, manufacture, and operational deployment of small nuclear bombs, no less, two of which fitted under the wing of the Scorpion, intended for detonation amongst the mass of non-existent Soviet bombers! What the Canadian and the Alaskans thought of this prospect is not recorded. As a piece of spin, this bomber threat ranks at least with Saddam Hussein's "weapons of mass destruction," Y2K, and a President who did now know what a sex act was.

5   Medaris, p 45.

6   Medaris, p 48.

7   Simon and Schuster, 1956, p 191.

8   Ruppelt, p 217.

9   Ruppelt, p 217.

10 Ruppelt, p 218.

11 Hall and Connors, p 146.

12 Ruppelt, p 220.

13 Ruppelt, p 222.

14 For a detailed discussion of Landy's involvement with UFOs, see Condon, p 104.

15 Hall and Connors, p 149.

16 In January 1947, Ramey, with a distinguished war record, assumed full command of the 8th Army Air Force with his HQ at Fort Worth. He took over from General McMullen, who became deputy chief of staff of the Strategic Air Command under Gen. George Kenney. Under Ramey's direct command was the 509th Bomb Group based at Roswell. As early as June 30, 1947, Ramey and his Intelligence chief were giving press interviews and debunking the new "flying saucer" phenomenon. But the saucers as usual, were to have the last laugh.

On July 6, 1947, Ramey spent all day attending an air show in his home town of Denton, Texas (and probably visiting relatives). Meanwhile, back in Fort Worth with Ramey away from the base, his chief of staff, Brig. Gen. Thomas Dubose, said he first learned of the find at Roswell by phone from SAC acting chief of staff Gen. McMullen. According to Dubose, McMullen ordered debris samples flown immediately to Washington by "colonel courier," first stopping in Fort Worth. The whole operation was carried out under the strictest secrecy, said

Notes

Dubose. McMullen ordered him not to tell anyone, not even Ramey. The infamous Roswell base flying disk press release occurred on July 8, 1947, and Ramey subsequent debunking the fragments found as bits from a "weather balloon." According to Dubose, McMullen ordered the cover-up in another phone call to Dubose from Washington. Both Dubose and Roswell Intelligence chief Jesse Marcel said the weather balloon was not what Marcel brought from Roswell, being nothing but a cover story to get rid of the press. (Information drawn from [**w**] http://roswellproof.homestead.com/Ramey_info ~ ns4.html)

17 For General Samford's biography, see [**w**] www.af.mil/bio/bio_7019.shtml

18 General Nathan F. Twining was appointed commanding general of the Air Materiel Command at Wright-Patterson Air Force Base in December of 1945. In October 10, 1950, he was appointed Vice Chief of Staff of the Air Force. This made General Twining the senior military adviser to the President (Harry Truman), and the Secretary of Defence (Charles E. Wilson). Concerning Roswell, the official USAF statement was that the debris recovered from the Roswell crash on July 8, 1947, was just a "weather balloon." However, a secret memorandum written by General Nathan Twining on September 23, 1947, suggests otherwise. "It is the opinion that the phenomenon reported is something real and not visionary or fictitious. There are objects probably approximating the shape of a disc, of such appreciable size as to appear to be as large as man-made aircraft." These comments have caused much argument and controversy. They are claimed by many to be forgeries, although this is disputed by such authorities as Stanton Friedman, author of *Crash at Corona* and *Top Secret/Majic*. For a summary of the negative arguments, see [**w**] www.roswellfiles.com/storytellers/Friedman.htm

19 Keyhoe, *Flying Saucers from Outer Space*, p 78.

20 For the complete details of the conference word for word, researcher Hall and Connors include the full text as Appendix III of *Summer of the Saucers*.

21 See *City of Revelation* by John Michell, Ballantine Books, 1973.

22 See *All Done With Mirrors* by John Neal, Secret Academy, 2000 [**e**] johnneal@secretacademy.com this being "An Exploration of Measure, Proportion, Ratio and Number."

23 Hall and Connors, p 267.

24 The connection between gravity and electromagnetic waves remains an open question in theoretical physics.

25 The guidance system of these ghost missiles is even more impressive. In Samford's time ground-control for airborne guidance was in its infancy, and analogue, not digital. Both the transistor and the integrating inertial accelerometer were only just out of the laboratories, and vacuum-tube electronics were the only things available for transmitted "guidance" of any kind, defined as moving the control surfaces of the aerofoil by radio command.

Vacuum-tube electronics were almost impossible to miniaturise. They entailed heater-filament batteries, various transformers and capacitors, diodes, and resistors, many of which these in those days were as thick as a thumb. In 1950, White Sands was only just beginning to test-fire the very earliest much-troubled prototypes of only semi-guided battlefield missiles, as distinct from the far better progress with purely ballistic missiles, such as the re-engineered V2. It can be said for a certainty that in 1952, at the time of the press conference, there was not a single guided missile proper in the entire operational inventory of the US armed services, although a few crude prototypes had been flown with mixed results. The only guided missile proper at this time was in a museum. This was the very advanced air-launched German cruise-missile, the Henschel 293 "Fritz X." This TV-guided anti-shipping weapon was first and last seen in action in the Mediterranean in late 1944, when it was successfully used against allied shipping.

26 Hall and Connors, p 279.
27 Hall and Connors, p 147.
28 *Top Secret/Majic*, Marlowe & Company, 1996.
29 Hall and Connors, p 279.
30 Hall and Connors, p 279.
31 Ruppelt, p 223.
32 Ruppelt, pp 223-224
33 Ruppelt, p 224.
34 Ruppelt, pp 225-226.

Also by Colin Bennett from Headpress

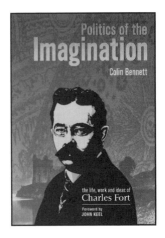

ISBN **1-900486-20-2**

176pp / Illustrated

UK **£12.99**
US **$19.95**

**Anomalist Award
for
Best Biography 2002**

POLITICS OF THE IMAGINATION

The Life, Work and Ideas of Charles Fort

by Colin Bennett

Born in Albany, New York, in 1874, Charles Fort spent almost his entire life searching through periodicals in the New York Public Library and the British Museum, compiling evidence to show that science was a mere façade that concealed as much as it claimed to have discovered. The "foe of science" is how the *New York Times* described Fort in its obituary…

Foreword by John Keel (author of *The Mothman Prophecies*).

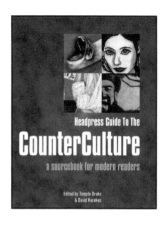